THE LEARNED BLACKSMITH

MERLE CURTI

THE LEARNED BLACKSMITH

Your faithful friend.
Elihu Burritt.

THE LEARNED BLACKSMITH

The Letters and Journals
of Elihu Burritt

By

MERLE CURTI
DWIGHT W. MORROW PROFESSOR OF HISTORY, SMITH COLLEGE

NEW YORK

WILSON-ERICKSON

INCORPORATED

1937

COPYRIGHT, 1937, BY
WILSON-ERICKSON, INC.

DESIGNED BY GEO. E. NEUHEDEL

PRINTED IN THE UNITED STATES OF AMERICA
BY THE COLONIAL PRESS INC., CLINTON, MASS.

To Arthur L. Weatherly,

One of the few leaders in the peace movement who at the cost of great personal sacrifice remained true to their peace principles throughout the world war.

ACKNOWLEDGMENTS

FOR several years I have been collecting Burritt material. With the exception of three letters and a few extracts from Burritt's *Journals* which appeared in peace periodicals that are now very rare, the material in this volume has never before been printed. Not all the unpublished letters that I have seen are included in this volume; but those that I have selected, and the passages from the *Journals,* are representative of Burritt's thought, activities and character. Burritt's letters, and selections from his *Journals,* are here printed exactly as he wrote them, except that the very few instances of misspelling or wrong word order which are quite obviously slips of the pen have been corrected. For example, where a proper name is usually spelled correctly in the manuscripts, but in one place is misspelled, that misspelling has been corrected. Except for such cases the policy has been to reproduce all the abbreviations and errors, including faults of punctuation, as in the original manuscript. Since this volume was completed, I have learned of a collection of eighty unpublished letters written by Burritt to one of his Quaker helpers in England during the years 1848 to 1855. This collection, which is at present in the hands of Mr. S. Graveson, will be deposited in the Library of Friends House in London.

I am especially grateful to Miss Greta Brown and the Trustees of the Library of the Institute of New Britain for permission to include the Burritt letters and selections from the *Journals* of Burritt in the possession of the Institute. Dr. Arthur Deerin Call, Secretary of the

American Peace Society in Washington, D. C., kindly gave permission to use the letters of Burritt deposited in the archives of the Society. Dr. Harry Dana put at my disposal the Burritt letters in the Longfellow papers in Craigie House, Cambridge. I am also very grateful to the Harvard College Library for permission to use the letters of Burritt in the Charles Sumner papers; to the Library of Syracuse University for permission to include letters in the Gerrit Smith Miller Collection; to the Library of Oberlin College, Friends House, London, the Library of the Hague Peace Palace, the Massachusetts Historical Society, the Henry E. Huntington Library and Art Gallery, the Library of Congress and the Department of State for permission to include Burritt letters in their possession. The portion of the letter from Burritt to Longfellow which was printed in Samuel Longfellow's *Life of Henry Wadsworth Longfellow* is included by permission of the Houghton Mifflin Company.

I wish to express my appreciation for courtesies extended by Mrs. Lyra Trueblood Wolkins, Dr. Thomas P. Martin, Mr. Manning Hawthorne, Dr. Paul Buck, Mr. John L. Nickalls, Mr. Julian Fowler, and Dr. W. F. Galpin. I am very grateful to Miss Ruth Yates, Mrs. Louis Hunter, and, especially, to Mr. Lawrence Crooks for help in checking the text with photostats or the original documents; to Miss Pauline Moor and Miss Lillian Levin for typing the manuscript; to Miss Mary Pardee Allison for proofreading; and to my wife for many helpful suggestions.

MERLE CURTI

CONTENTS

THE LEARNED BLACKSMITH

CHAPTER I

A SELF-MADE MAN

*E*LIHU BURRITT was a poor boy. Like other boys a hundred years ago, he gloried in the idea of self-improvement, and like many of his contemporaries he became a self-made man. But it was not worldly riches that he made. His lifelong ideal was to serve mankind, to promote human brotherhood, and he was never tempted to take another path. Unlike most Americans, he had no ambition to rise above the working class from which he came.

On December 8, 1810 Elihu Burritt was born in the little village of New Britain, Connecticut. His father, for whom he was named, had been a common soldier in the Revolution. With great difficulty he eked out a narrow living for his wife, Elizabeth Hinsdale Burritt, and his ten children, by cultivating a few rocky, barren acres of soil and by plying his trade of shoemaking. Neighbors respected this man for his scrupulous honesty and uprightness and for his willingness to share what little he had with those worse off than himself. But in their estimation his active and speculative mind was impractical and led him into many ill-timed adventures, so that much of the brunt of looking out for the family fell on his wife, a pious woman and a model of self-sacrifice and devotion. Elihu resembled his parents in many respects.

Burritt's boyhood was one of hardship and deprivation. True, there were a few simple pleasures. He saw

1

with a boy's eyes the speckled trout sporting in the meadow brook, and sometimes found an opportunity to go fishing or to take part in nutting expeditions. With the other boys of the village he took delight in listening to the stories of veterans of the Revolutionary War, and in watching the militia parade on the village green on training days. But this solemn youngster found the greatest satisfaction in reading warlike stories in the Bible and in rereading the handful of religious books and historical works in the library of the parish church.

His child's heart revolted at every kind of injustice. One day—he was fourteen—the schoolmaster, exhausted by the unruliness of his students, declared that any pupil detected in whispering was to take the ferrule and stand in the corner until he observed some like offender, to whom he could surrender its keeping. The pupil who should have the ferrule in his possession at the moment of dismissal would be punished for all the offenders that afternoon. A few minutes before school closed a boy was mean enough to tempt a girl who was a great favorite to whisper, and consequently she stood to be penalized for all the rest. This was more than Elihu Burritt could endure: he whispered on purpose to save her from becoming the "recipient of forty blows save one."

The death of his father and the poverty of the family made it impossible for Elihu to obtain more than the most meager schooling. He became an apprentice to Samuel Booth, the village blacksmith. This one-legged man was exemplary for his piety and his benevolence and doubtless confirmed the warmhearted impulses of his apprentice. While at work in the smithy Elihu placed Thomson's *Seasons*, a book of romantic poetry, against the forge chimney and, as the iron was heating and the sparks flying, "took short sips of its beauty." But for the most part he occupied his mind with all sorts of mental feats, such as measuring the distance around the earth in barleycorns. He took great delight in learning Latin and Greek verbs which he could conjugate in his mind as his arms and hands were busy at the forge. So insatiable was his thirst for knowledge that he acquired a remarkable faculty for cultivating his mind as he worked and after he went home at night. When he was twenty-two he had become so fascinated by the family resemblances between Latin, Greek, French and his mother tongue that he managed to take three months from his work at the smithy in order to pursue, at New Haven, the study of these languages and Spanish, Italian, German and Hebrew as well. Although he lived in the shadow of Yale, he modestly thought it would be unbecoming for a young man of twenty-two to seek the aid of scholars in acquiring a rudimentary knowledge of Greek and Hebrew, so he made no effort to find a tutor.

Too close application to his studies contributed to a breakdown in health. The young blacksmith tried his hand at school-teaching and at storekeeping. When the panic of 1837 paralyzed business and swept away his meager savings he decided to start life over again in new surroundings. Perhaps, even, he could find work as a sailor on some ship bound for Europe, and there obtain such works in the modern and Oriental languages as he had been unable to acquire at New Haven. Almost penniless, he started out on foot. At Worcester, some hundred miles from New Britain, he heard of the Antiquarian Society, and found that he could borrow grammars and lexicons. So he secured work at a foundry, and dug deep into the more difficult languages. Before long he had composed a letter in the Celto-Breton tongue which he sent to the Royal Antiquarian Society in France. A few months later, as he stood in his leather work-apron at the forge, his gray-blue eyes lighted up as he was handed a large volume, bearing the seal of the learned French society, and a letter testifying to the correctness of his composition.

As the months and years passed the young blacksmith made himself more or less acquainted with all the languages of Europe and with several of Asia, including Hebrew, Chaldaic, Samaritan and Ethiopic. Anxious to turn his knowledge to some practical account and to supplement his meager earnings of twenty-five cents a day, he solicited an opportunity to make translations. He had no idea that it would involve any publicity, and was "horrified and astounded" when he read that Governor Edward Everett had, in an address at a Teachers Institute at Taunton, referred to his remarkable attainments. To his surprise and chagrin this excessively modest youth, who was so shy that at twenty-one he still scarcely "dared look a schoolgirl in the face," found himself suddenly acclaimed "the learned blacksmith." The public was the more ready to accept this title by reason of his high, receding forehead, his deeply set, steady, keen eyes, his thin visage, his fair complexion and the hectic glow in his cheeks, and his strong muscles and powerful hands.[1]

[1] The Swedish novelist, Fredrika Bremer, met Burritt at about this time, and described him as "a very tall and strong-limbed man with an unusually lofty forehead, large, beautiful eyes, and predominatingly handsome and strong features—a man who would excite attention in any company whatever, not only for his figure but for the expression of singular mildness and human love which marks his countenance." *America of the Fifties: Letters of Fredrika Bremer*, selected and edited by Adolph B. Benson (N. Y., 1924), pp. 41-42.

Governor Everett invited the blacksmith to dinner, and, in behalf of several men of wealth, offered him all the advantages for further study which Harvard University afforded. Longfellow generously suggested that he would be glad to aid him, in every way, during his proposed residence at Cambridge. Burritt chose, however, to continue his linguistic work in combination with manual labor, and without teachers. Hard toil he regarded as indispensable to health and happiness, and he had no desire to take flight in the secluded life of a scholar. He preferred, as he told Longfellow, "to stand in the ranks of the workingmen of New England, and beckon them onward and upward . . . to the full stature of intellectual men." [2] In view of the fact that most American workingmen have always been anxious to rise from their class, this loyalty on the part of the blacksmith of New Britain is all the more noteworthy. Here was a self-made man who meant to devote his talents to values other than those of worldly success.

In the midst of his unremitting toil Burritt edited a little monthly magazine, *The Literary Geminae*. Half of it was made up of selected writings in French; the other half of articles and translations from his own pen. This first literary venture, however, did not outlive the year.

Meanwhile, without entirely abandoning his work in the foundry, Burritt accepted invitations to talk on the lecture platform.[3] The idea of self-culture was in the

---

[2] E. W. Bailey, "Elihu Burritt," *Southern Literary Messenger*, Vol. VI, (March, 1840), pp. 201 ff.; Vol. IX (April, 1843), pp. 234 ff. See also Burritt's letter to Longfellow in Samuel Longfellow's *Life of Henry Wadsworth Longfellow* (Boston, 1886), Vol. II, p. 363.

[3] An interesting parallel to the career of Elihu Burritt is that of Robert Collyer, an English blacksmith who migrated to America in 1850, and, through self-education, became a distinguished Unitarian minister and

air: in 1838 William Ellery Channing had elaborated
this concept in great detail in an address to manual
workers in Boston, [4] and it had been re-echoed from in-
numerable lecture platforms and in dozens of periodicals. Elihu Burritt, "the learned blacksmith," was, of
course, a perfect example of self-culture, and it was the
natural theme for his first lecture, "Application and
Genius." In this address the theory was advanced that
genius is made, not inherited; that strong motives, persistent will and unflagging devotion and application are
the chief factors in intellectual achievement. Burritt
hoped that this lecture, which he gave some sixty times in
one season, might inspire other young workingmen to
cultivate their minds as he had done.

But Elihu Burritt was too sensitive and too vigorous
a man to find satisfaction in lecturing to young artisans
on self-culture; too much alive to be occupied with the
syntax of dead languages. True, almost everyone attached great importance to knowledge for the mere sake
of knowledge. In many eyes it was an end in itself. Nothing had been more natural than for this young blacksmith to assume that the acquisition of learning, however unrelated it was to his work and life, was a worthy
value, that it toughened the mind, strengthened the character, and enriched the heart. Few indeed were the scholars who thought of knowledge which was unrelated to
life as sterile. Channing, to be sure, had said in his address on self-culture that one of its chief ends was to fit
us for action, "to train us to firmness of purpose and to
fruitfulness of resource in common life." We do not

friend of the underprivileged. John Haynes Holmes, *The Life and Letters of
Robert Collyer 1823-1912* (N. Y., 1917).

[4] *The Works of William E. Channing, D.D.* (Boston, 1886), pp. 12-36.

know whether Burritt was familiar with this lecture of the great Unitarian, or not. But in any case he began to ask himself whether languages were not, after all, chiefly important as vehicles for ideas and thoughts. Gradually he came to see that "there was something to live for besides the mere gratification of a desire to learn—that there were words to be spoken with the living tongue and earnest heart for great principles of truth and righteousness." To the great humanitarian crusades of the day, therefore, Burritt became increasingly responsive. Temperance, [5] the abolition of slavery, and world peace, as well as the elevation of the working class, found in him a staunch friend.

[5] For one of Burritt's characteristic temperance sketches see "The Influence of the Drunkard" in *Miscellaneous Writings*, pp. 96-97. Burritt also supported "the Maine law' which made illegal the sale of intoxicating beverages. See *Bond of Brotherhood*, new series, no. 59, June, 1855, p 175

Worcester, June 15th, 1839

Mrs. L. H. Sigourney [6]
Dear Madame,

I take the liberty of sending you a copy of the first number of a new periodical which I have just commenced, under the title of "The Literary Geminae"; a publication which, I hope and design, shall add to the facilities of the young ladies and gentlemen of New England, for their acquisition of the French language.

I send it to you, not with an expectation so sanguine, as to suppose that it could possibly contribute to your personal entertainment, but rather as an evidence, that I do not feel myself warranted to commence or continue a publication which has for its avowed object, the mental and moral improvement of the young, without first soliciting and securing the approbation of *one* whose very name is identified with all that tends to the salutary cultivation of the minds and hearts of the youth of our country. And I beg that you recognize it also as a humble tribute of veneration and respect, from one who is happy and proud to say of *your* native state: "I was born there." With these sentiments, and others more expressive of my ardent wishes for your peace and prosperity,

I am, Dear Madame,
Yours most Obed" and most
Respectfully

Elihu Burritt

BURRITT MSS.
Library of the Institute of New Britain

[6] Mrs. Sigourney was a poet who lived at Hartford, Connecticut.

WORCESTER Dec. 1st 1840

Prof H. W. Longfellow
My Dear Sir

I have just returned from Connecticut, whither I have been to spend Thanksgiving and to eat a little of my good old mother's chicken-pie and to participate in the other interesting exercises of the occasion. I left Worcester the morning of the same day that your very kind and interesting letter was dated; a circumstance which I hope will plead for my seeming delay in returning you an answer. Your very kind invitation to take up my residence in Cambridge is to me a very interesting proposition; and I wish, My Dear Sir, that I could tell you how gratefully I am affected at your benevolent interest in my pursuits. I have long thought that if I could obtain access to the library of Harvard University, it would be preferable to remaining here. Still I feel much attached to Worcester, and it would seem like leaving the best home I have, to go from this place; although I doubt not that I should meet with friendship elsewhere. I have a job of work which I hope to complete in the course of four weeks, when I shall be at liberty from any engagement. In the meantime, I mean to avail myself of your invitation to visit Cambridge, this week or next, if I can get away—and ascertain if I can find a boarding-place and other requisites for a residence in Cambridge. There is one thing though—may I bring my hammer with me? must I *sink* that altogether? I can assure you, that my hammer is as much predisposed to *swim* on the top of all my ideas, as was the axe to float on the surface of the water at the touch of the prophet.

I thank you from my whole heart for your kind proffer of pecuniary assistance in prosecuting my studies. Having acquired the habit of regarding my literary pursuits as matters of mere recreation, and not allowing myself to expect from them anything but a species of transient gratification, I have long ago resolved to make them entirely subservient to the more necessary and important avocations of life, and not to indulge them at the expense of valuable time or the price of labor. With this view, I have always confined my "literary leisure" to those unoccupied hours of the day *when no man can work*; thus associating whatever benefit or pleasure I may derive from my studies, with the idea of a prerequisite of relaxation from manual labor. And I can assure you, Sir, that each of these two departments of my occupations gives a lively zest to the other. When I return at evening to my little chamber, with the consciousness of having performed a full day's labor, I set down at my desk and commune with my little shelf of books with a relish that indeed makes it a recreation. And in the morning, after having blown out my morning lamp, I resume my hammer with an equal relish, and ply it with such force and effect as give strength to my arm, make the coarsest and commonest fare more delicious than the viands of princes, sweeten my repose—and procure me all the gratifications of industry. But what is paramount to every other consideration is, that my physical constitution will admit of no suspension of athletic exercise, which, in whatever situation I may be placed, I never could resist my inclination to seek in honest and honorable manual labor. Then there is another thing:—I am not *odd*, I affect no singularity, no excentricity [*sic*];—but still I am ambitious —everybody is ambitious, and I am particularly so to stand in the ranks of the working-men of New England and beg and beckon them onward and upward, if I can, into the full stature of *intellectual men*. I feel that I shall come short of this influence or object, immeasurably short of it in everything but my intention and hope. But if Providence should spare my life and intellectual ability, I shall covet no higher human reward for any attainment I may make in literature or science, than the satisfaction of having stood in the lot of the laboring man. I cannot but anticipate one result from this course, which is, that I shall not only procure thereby a comfortable subsistence, but also the means of intellectual improvement. Had I not embarked last year in a foolhardy enterprise of publishing a periodical, I should have at this moment a pleasant competence for honest purposes. I assure you I am not an *amateur* working man. With my own hands I earned last year nearly $1000, besides some little time devoted to my magazine. About $600 of this I lost by that publication, but feel now *on my feet again*. If I should take up my residence in Cambridge, I trust it would not be necessary to interrupt my usual course. My business is extremely pressing just at this time, but I mean to visit Cambridge the first pleasant day, when I hope to tell you face to face how much and how sincerely I am Yours, etc.,

ELIHU BURRITT.

LONGFELLOW MSS.
Craigie House
[Printed in part in the *Life of Henry Wadsworth Longfellow*, edited by Samuel Longfellow (2 volumes, Boston, 1886), Vol. I, pp. 363-364]

[MS. JOURNALS] [7]

[Worcester, Mass.] Saturday, Aug. 21, 1841.

Very warm, faint weather; feel sweaty and worn out; have been absent from my work only two days during the last five months. Congress has passed the great Bankrupt Bill,[8] which a few days ago they laid upon the table for the session. Studied Armenian. Have forged 11 hours.

[7] All of the selections from Burritt's *Journals* are taken from the manuscripts in the Library of the Institute of New Britain.
[8] *Statutes at Large*, v. 440, 614. This act, like that of 1800, proved unsatisfactory in many respects and was later repealed.

Monday, [Aug.] 23rd [1841]

Head heavy; feel indisposed to study; the time between sunrise and breakfast very short. Went to the shop; employers told me that they could find no more work for me at present; none to be had in the neighborhood. I cannot bring my mind to think of studying while my means of support are precarious. Commenced a letter to Dr Peters,[9] New York, requesting him to ask the publishers of the *Observer* and *Evangelist,* if they could not pay me a cent a line for such articles as I might contribute to their papers. An article once a week would nearly pay my board which would make me feel rich. Have forged 8 pruning hooks, which I may sell next spring. Captain Holdbrook delivered a most interesting lecture on temperance this evening.[10]

Tuesday, Aug. 24 [1841]

Feel depressed in spirits; disinclined to study while in a state of anxiety about getting work. . . .

Thursday, Aug. 26 [1841]

Studied Ethiopic one hour. I work for the sake of working. During the afternoon I staid in the shop with my coat and vest off, merely to feel myself in my usual preparation for labor. I cannot occupy this leisure studying; there is a constant uneasiness in my mind which renders me unable to compose my thoughts upon any literary pursuits. My mind is now running upon the plan of taking a school in Nov. The idea of leaving Worcester becomes daily more unpleasant.

Saturday, Aug. 28 [1841]

Feel in that state of suspense that disinclines me for study and almost everything else. If I do not hear from

[9] Absalom Peters (1793-1869), a Presbyterian minister and secretary of the American Home Missionary Society, was at this time editor of the *American Eclectic.*

[10] For the early history of the temperance movement see John Krout, *Origins of Prohibition* (N. Y., 1925).

New York by next Monday, I must lay out a new course of life. In mingling so many literary pursuits with my manual occupations, I begin to feel that I have been chasing a shadow. I cannot but regret that I have not pursued my trade more exclusively. . .

Friday, Sept. 22 [1841]

Wrote half of the day. Hired a forge and began to prepare for making garden utensils. I have given up the idea of removing from Worcester this fall. My money is all gone, and if I should be sick I should be in an unpleasant predicament. I have relinquished the hope of obtaining anything by my pen; such a hope is a delusive phantom as thousands have realized whose claims upon it were stronger than mine. . . . .

WORCESTER, September 22, 1841

Rev Heman Humphrey, D. D.[11]

Honored Sir:—I take this opportunity of tendering to you, good sir, and to the Faculty of Amherst College, my most grateful acknowledgements for the flattering testimonial of your consideration which you have been pleased to confer upon me. You may easily conceive, Sir, that I could not but be deeply affected at the reception of such an honorable and unsolicited mark of distinction. Nor need I say that I prize it richly, as an evidence not of *merit*, but of *debt* to a generous public, which will inspire me to more assiduous exertions in future. I accept it with inexpressible sentiments of pleasure, not as a *personal* honor, but as a pledge of encouragement, on your part, Gent, given to the young working men of New England, for whom I am living and for whom I shall die. It is with them that I desire to share *this* honor, and all others that may attend my future career;

[11] Heman Humphrey (1779-1861), Congregational clergyman and president of Amherst College. The College had recently honored Burritt with a diploma.

and my earthly ambition will have attained its goal, when I shall have left them some feeble waymarks to the temple of knowledge and of virtue.

I hope these sentiments, Gent, will enable you to appreciate the sincerity of my gratitude, and to accept the assurances of respect and reverence with which I am

Your Humble Servant,—ELIHU BURRITT

[This letter was copied in his
Journal, Sept. 22, 1841]

[MS. JOURNALS]

Thursday, Oct. 7th [1841]

Read Ethiopic 1 hour; wrote 1 hour upon a subject of which I intend to make a lecture, viz. "Is Roman patriotism or Christian philanthropy most congenial to the Republican principle?" Got trusted for 30 pounds of cast steel to make my garden hoes of. Went to the library and read 2-½ hours. Forged from 1 to 5 P. M. Anti-Slavery Convention in the evening; listened to the most thrilling and powerful speeches. Mr. Leavitt [12] of New York made a speech worthy of a statesman and orator, a scholar and Christian. The crisis is at hand; they have seized upon the right plan to meet the emergency. The institution of slavery has given a direction to almost every political question; it has overshadowed all our institutions; it militates against every republican principle; it renders our government an anomaly to the world. The people of New England have been enjoined by every moral consideration to keep it from mingling with politics, as if it was a cause too holy to be involved in political action. Never was a more delusive humbug foisted upon the credulity of our northern freemen than this.

---

[12] Joshua Leavitt (1794–1873), clergyman, reformer, pioneer abolitionist, editor of *The Emancipator* and later of *The Independent*.

Monday, Oct. 25 [1841]

Forged all day; my job is rather a hard one, but I feel grateful for anything to do by which I can earn a little. Sent two letters to Rev Mr Bailey,[13] one of which contained my article for the *Patriarch*. Received an invitation from Brooklyn, New York, to lecture before their Lyceum, which makes nine engagements of that kind for the coming season.

Saturday, [Oct.] 15 [1842]

Read a chapter in Gaelic, then resumed my writing on my lecture, which progresses at the rate of one page a day. Sent off a letter to Mrs. A. M. Whetmore, Sec. Half Orphan Asylum New York, asking if a temperance lecture would not answer their turn; as I have nothing on hand just now of another character. In the afternoon I found my head growing heavy, and therefore girded on my apron and forged till tea time. Mr Sayles, a suffrage exile from Rhode Island,[14] gave an exposé of that question in the evening, which was listened to with great interest and attention by a very numerous audience of both parties. At first the Whigs thought it was to be a partisan affair to play into the hands of their opponents, and therefore attended quite numerously in order to throw some impediment in the way. They tried to get a chairman of the meeting for this purpose, but lost it being outvoted by their opponents. Mr Sayles is a small sentimental exquisite to look to, but possessing much talent. He gave a clear and concise history of the Rhode Island question of the right of suffrage; and, if all he said was true, the Charter party had been really oppressive and insolent

[13] Dr. Rufus William Bailey (1793-1863), antislavery Congregational clergyman and president of Austin College, Texas. Dr. Bailey was at this time editor of the *Patriarch*, a moral-religious periodical published in New York.

[14] The Dorr War was a struggle, led by Thomas Dorr, for extending the suffrage. Class feeling ran high, and the movement was in many respects comparable to an incipient war. See A. M. Mowry, "The Constitutional Controversy in Rhode Island in 1841," in *Am. Hist. Asso. Annual Report for 1894* (Washington, 1895), pp. 361-370.

to the people. One fact has been fully demonstrated by their conduct, which is, that the voluntary abdication of power requires considerable virtue in man individually or collectively.

Tuesday, [Oct.] 25 [1842]

. . . . At 9-½ I took the stage for Worcester, having for a fellow-passenger Gen. Carpenter of R. I. with whom I had a long conversation upon the suffrage question. There is no doubt but that the *people* were in the right, and took the only way to assert it. For more than 40 years they have been petitioning the Charter Legislature for a slight extension of the right of suffrage, and these petitions have been treated with insolent ridicule and indifference; nor did they manifest the least inclination to meet the people with any alleviation of the grievance; nor would they have done it to this day unless they had been forced to it by an insurrection.

Wednesday 14 [Feb., 1843]

. . . Took the stage for North Hampton, where, after much delay on account of the roads, I arrived at 3 P.M. Took lodgings at the Mansion House, an excellent establishment. I immediately set out on foot to visit Prof Adam, who is at the head of a kind of transcendental community about 2 miles west of the village of North Hampton.[15] After a fatiguing walk in the deep snow, I reached the establishment, and was chagrined to find that Mr. Adam was not at home. My journey however was not lost, for it procured me an ocular demonstration how utterly impracticable, unnatural, visionary & absurd was this chimerical species of Association. Never did I see a place where more self-denial & sacrifice of personal comfort, rights, & privileges seemed requisite than here. In a large abandoned silk factory, thinly parti-

[15] W. A. Hinds, *American Communities and Co-operative Colonies* (Chicago, 1908), pp. 276–280; J. H. Noyes, *History of American Socialisms* (Phila., 1870), pp. 154–160.

tioned off into rooms larger than cells, nearly a hundred amateurs of this new social system had come together by a species of mutual attraction, as they would call it. Here, aloof from the world, they flatter themselves that they are going to develop a new character in human nature and society, and show the age what a perfect being man may be when left to the unrestricted impulse & tendencies of his own propensities & passions. Here all distinctions of rank & occupation are to be abolished. All are to be alternately teachers, preachers & artisans. With no practicable ideas of business, or mechanical art, they are going to compete with shrewd individual genius & enterprise. The apartments I visited were cold, comfortless & untidy. Accomplished ladies who had left good homes & the luxuries of refined life, were here surrounded by their half abandoned children, trying to learn the trade of some factory operative, in a room roughly & thinly partitioned off with unplaned, upright boards, whose open joints were concealed in the inner side by coarse paper pasted over them. This is the drawing, library, dressing and working room, with all the respective provisions for such a character, scattered around in slattern profusion & negligence.

Mr. Mock, the president (for they are obliged to have some officers after all) went with me to Prof. Adam's, and introduced me to his family, comprising his wife & three daughters who have been bred & brought up in affluence & whom I found engaged in occupations, which once, while residing in India, were performed for them by 18 servants. I spent an hour with them very pleasantly & profitably for they showed me the Professor's library, which contained a large collection of oriental works, embracing lexicons & grammars of the Persian, Bengalee & Hindostanee etc. I intend to negotiate with him for these books for I feel that I must own the books that I need of this kind, instead of borrowing them. Returned to the hotel tired & cold, and spent the evening pleasantly with several gentlemen whom I met there. Among these was the celebrated Dr Graham,[16] who pressed me to stay another day and lecture before the citizens of North Hampton; which I finally agreed to do. I met here also a Mr Hotchkiss, a merchant from New Haven, a very worthy, intelligent & pious man, whose company & conversation were interesting. My former pupil, Paul W. Allen is here also, and has acquired the soubriquet of *Doctor*, having been studying that profession for the last year. He has been lecturing upon physiology & the pathology of Drunkenness in the villages of the Connecticut.

Thursday 15 [Feb., 1843]

A clear, cold morning; after breakfast, I called upon Dr Graham, who is very enthusiastically fond of metaphysics, and is an original genius withall. He has been engaged in writing upon the moral philosophy of the Scriptures, and has already produced two volumes upon the subject. He has an interesting family, and is himself much of a gentleman. While we were engaged in conversation, several young ladies & gentlemen came in, and delighted us with several exquisitely well executed tunes. One of the ladies, Miss Phelps, from Greenfield, a beautiful creature, sang & played with a voice & style I hardly ever heard surpassed. Mr Hotchkiss carried me about the village in his sleigh, and returning to the hotel, I found an invitation to take tea with Judge Lyman, who was chairman at the Hartford Convention. He is truly a gentleman of the old school; one of those ripe, hale, benign old men who look so blooming in the Indian summer of age. He has two beautiful daughters at home, one of whom I met at Worcester. I passed an agreeable hour with them, and went with them to the lecture room, which was well filled. I went through with my lecture with much animation, and received the most respectful attention

[16] Dr. Sylvester Graham (1794-1851), advocate of temperance and noted health reformer for whom "graham bread" was named.

from the audience. Dr Graham took me with him to a party at Mrs J. Clarke's, where I found a brilliant company assembled, who spent the evening in music & dancing. Miss Phelps was the belle of the evening, & sang, played & danced to the fascination of all. I was urged to stay another day, & visit Miss Dwights seminary, but was obliged to decline.

[Worcester] Wed. April 26, 1843

I finished my Danish document to my great satisfaction and relief. I have laboured upon it a fortnight constantly, and if I get nothing for my labor but the ability to translate Danish and German manuscripts I shall deem myself rewarded. Forged in the afternoon and attended our conference meeting in the evening.

Monday, May 1st [1843]

The storm increased almost to a tempest this morning. Read Arabic and translated from the German until noon; worked upon my hoes [17] till tea time, and then resumed my translation which I worked upon till 10.

Worcester, May 17, 1843

Messers Little Brown:

As every thing relating to the early history of this country seems to assume an increasing interest I venture to submit to your consideration a proposition to translate, from the Spanish, La Vega *History of Florida*,[18] embracing a description of the country, its natural productions, the customs & character of the Indians; also a detailed account of the occupation and conquest of the country by Hernando de Soto, with all his discoveries and adventures, battles with

[17] Burritt was temporarily engaged in forging garden hoes as a means of livelihood.

[18] Garcilasso de la Vega's *Florida* was published as part of *Conquesta del nuevo mondo* (Madrid, 1722-1723).

the natives, &c. La Vega's great work, *The Royal Commentaries on Peru* was translated in 1628, but his History of Florida has never been rendered into English, to my knowledge. It would make an octavo vol. of about 400 pages which I would translate for 50 cts a page and take half the amount in such books as I need in collecting a small library. If the proposition should be deemed worthy of your notice, I should be happy to confer with you further upon the subject, at your pleasure and convenience.

Yours Very Respectfully,
Elihu Burritt

BURRITT MSS.
Library of the Institute of New Britain

[MS. JOURNALS]

Tuesday [May] 23 [1843]

Read Arabic and wrote a page on my Peace lecture. This indeed is snail-like progress, but if unremitting it will come to something in the end. I mean to keep up my courage and not give over on account of my poor facility of composition. In the afternoon I forged 5 hoes in 3 hours; spent the evening in my rooms.

[Boston] Wednesday [June] 28 [1843]

An extremely hot day; felt weak and feverish from my efforts last evening. There could not have been a worse time selected for lectures of this kind. I kept the house all day, and found a home like a fathers at the kind Mr Gilberts. I was treated as a son and brother by the family; which I shall always remember with gratitude. In the evening I delivered my new Peace lecture with all the effect I ever anticipated. It chained the audience for 1-½ hours, as well as any thing I ever delivered. Several of the first men of

Boston were present and testified their gratification in a very expressive manner. I intend to deliver it as often as opportunity opens, for I believe it may do good.

Monday [July] 17 [1843]

Read Gaelic, Alison,[19] and wrote a little on my lecture upon the *dignity* of Manual Labor. . . .

[Gardiner, Maine] Wednesday [August] 9 [1843]

. . . . Gardiner is quite a large town, full of vigorous energy, and engaged extensively in the Lumber business, commerce & manufactures. Shipbuilding is carried on along the Kennebec with much activity, and the bravest sons of the ocean hail from Maine . . . Took up my lodgings with Capt Berry, a retired sea-captain, a warm hearted, polite & affable gentleman. He took me to the rooms of the Mechanics Institution, where I was introduced to delegates from every part of the State. They were all embarrassingly respectful, and treated me with a consideration which somewhat oppressed me.

Friday [August] 11 [1843]. . . . My efforts at Gardiner were rewarded with a corresponding liberality. For making a journey of 200 miles for the especial purpose of addressing their State Convention and the effort itself, they generously gave me $10 besides unanimously voting that I should give them a copy of my address, thus dispossessing me of a production which was the result of two months labor!

[Worcester, Mass.] Thursday [Sept.] 28 [1843]

Continued on my lecture as usual. Received a letter from Richmond Va. inviting me to lecture there next winter. I

[19] Probably Sir Archibald Alison's *History of Europe* (London, 1842).

have, however, about made up my mind not to make another journey South this season. I find the atmosphere of the Slave States is difficult to breathe and irritates my lungs. Sent away a letter to Manchester offering to lecture for them Nov. 2.

Julius Clarke spent the evening at my room when we tried to concoct some antislavery action. We have both resolved to espouse the cause of the Liberty Party this fall. I expect to lose some of my reputation, but I do not wish to retain any of it that is based on my support of a slaveholder.

Friday [Sept.] 29 [1843]

Clarke spent most of the forenoon with me talking over some plan of action for the cause of freedom. We discussed at large the feasibility of getting up a small antislavery paper to be sustained by the patronage & talent of Worcester County. Occupied most of the day in making preparations for a meeting of a few friends of the cause at my room in the evening. Succeeded in assembling about 10 of the old organization, including the Rev. Mr Hubbard the president of the Liberty party. We concluded to call a meeting of the Society next Monday evening to choose officers & transact other business. We also agreed to hire a man to procure subscriptions for the extra Emancipator,[20] and distribute antislavery tracts. We raised 6 dollars on the spot to purchase copies of the Emancipator for gratuitous circulation. Thus I have put my name to a work which may seriously affect my standing, but I will stand the hazard or die.

[Bangor, Maine] Thursday [Oct.] 19 [1843]

I have been dreadfully afflicted for nearly a week with a pain in the small of my back, so that I begin to apprehend it may be an affection of the spine. I hope that the unde-

[20] A Boston antislavery publication.

served mercy of God, which has so long watched over me, will not permit me to [be] scourged in the midst of my days with that hopeless malady. Wrote but little on account of my inability to sit. Shall not try to finish my new lecture [on labor] to deliver here, but give them my old one on Native Genius. Beales came in after dinner, when we had a long and animated conversation. Nothing can exceed the cordiality of my reception here among the Mechanics. They regard me as a champion of their profession, & I cannot but be deeply affected at their confidence & respect. Wrote a letter to Mr Hedge, of which the following is a copy. . . . Took tea with Mr Sawood who invited in nearly twenty members of the Mechanics association, to meet me just as if I were another Dickens. I began and related to them all my history from my youth up. They listened with the most absorbed attention to every word, & I returned to my lodgings deeply affected at their confidence & friendship & unbounded respect.

Saturday [Oct.] 21 [1843]

Wrote several letters & occupied the rest of the day receiving & making calls. Took tea at Mr Godfreys & met Prof Shepherd & several ladies. The Mechanics assembled in their hall to meet me as a particular guest. There was a large number present to whom I was introduced. After a free & animated conversation, they pressed me to give my experience. So I went behind the desk, and in the most awkward, incoherent, stammering manner, wandered over some of the principal points of my history. If I ever attempt to talk of *I* again I shall know it. I came home ashamed & humbled in my own estimation & theirs too I presume.

Tuesday [Oct.] 24 [1843]

Received several callers in the forenoon, which prevented my progress in copying off my lecture. Prof Smith was very kind & lavished upon me such expressions I shall long remember. Mr Walker, the Liberty candidate, promised to cooperate with our tract system, and endeavor to extend it over the whole region of the Penobscot. I had to dine out again, and on my return to my room, I found that I had hardly time enough to finish my lecture. I wrote with all my might till the very moment arrived for its delivery. I hastened to the church & commenced speaking while out of breath, which rendered my articulation laborious. The house was overflowing full, & the audience almost embarrassingly attentive. My lecture took as well as I expected, & I trust it will be useful & acceptable to the public. Returned to my room exhausted & afflicted with one of my nervous headaches.

[To Dr. Calvin Chapin,[21]
Hartford, Conn.]

[Worcester, Mass., Oct. 29, 1843]

Rev. & Dear Sir:

I venture to address you upon a subject in which your heart must take a lively interest. A few individuals of us, residing in different parts of New England, have associated ourselves into a society called the *New England Central Tract Association*, for the more general diffusion of light upon the subject of *slavery*, and the duties of the Christian citizen with regard to that evil. I have taken it upon my department of the work, to correspond with eminent clergymen & other literary men in this country, England, & Scotland, with the view to solicit the aid of their talents to this great enterprise. We are anxious to bring an entirely new force of talent into the field, by enlisting those eminent & philanthropic men who have hitherto been driven from the cause by that ferocious fanaticism, that would demolish all

---

[21] Calvin Chapin (1763–1851), a Hartford clergyman, was a pioneer in the temperance cause. Burritt copied this letter in his *Journal* under the date Oct. 29, 1843.

the hallowed institutions of religion in order to get at the evil of slavery.

We hope to secure for the year, 52 of the best writers of the country, each of whom shall furnish the matter for a powerful tract upon one of the infinite tendencies of that dreadful system of wrong, which is preying like a cancer of fire upon the constitution of this republic. We are confident that the united effort of such pens would invest the cause with a dignity and power it has never assumed before in this country. Such a phalanx of eminent men appearing suddenly in the field at this crisis of the struggle, would almost certainly ensure a conquest for humanity which would be remembered & celebrated among the future jubilees of the race. We are taking adequate measures to disseminate weekly and gratuitously, not only through every town in New England, but through every city & village in the free states of the Union. And, Sir, we pledge all the energy of our ability to bring whatever thoughts you may contribute in contact with 200,000 human minds susceptible of illumination from yours. What a volume will those 52 tracts make! *what an album for the race! what a book of remembrance* for the unchained myriads of bondmen to bind to their bosoms, as a record of those who remembered them while groaning in the prison house of bondage! To each of these writers we intend to present a bound volume of the 52 tracts, to be preserved by their children & posterity, who will grow prouder & prouder of such an evidence that their ancestor was one of the champions of justice & human freedom. In *that book* of *remembrance* will you not inscribe your name with a few thoughts & sentiments in behalf of the slave? Will you not, in the course of the year, prepare or condense from your manuscripts, matter sufficient for a tract of 4 pages, bearing upon any aspect of slavery you please to select? It will cost you but a few hours labor; but its effect may endure for ages, and generations of the free *rise up to call you blessed.*

[MS. JOURNALS]

[Worcester, Mass.] Monday [Nov.] 13 [1843]

To day was election, and an interesting day for the country. A large vote was cast, & the Liberty ticket advanced from 45 to 120. It was an interesting day to me; for at the Ballot box I broke away from the Whigs & voted for the Liberty of the Slave.

Boston, Feb. 21 1845

S. D. Hastings Esq [22]

My very Dear Sir:

I have been so occupied with engagements since I saw you, that I have not been able to write a letter to my dearest friend. I expect to start on my trip to Philadelphia next Monday, the 24th. I have assigned one week to myself in reaching your city; as I have two engagements on my way, one in Bridgeport, the other in New York. I think I shall arrive in Philadelphia on Saturday, March 1st; when I should be happy to accompany you home to your *villa* out of the city and spend the sabbath in your affectionate family circle. On Tuesday evening I should like to deliver my lecture on "LABOR" in some hall that may be conveniently situated. I shall throw myself entirely into your hands and follow unwaveringly your directions. I think your suggestion of putting the tickets for the first lecture at 25 cents, and for a more popular audience, at 12-½ cents, the best plan to be adopted. Now, friend Hastings, I know your unbounded kindness may incline you to speak some pleasant things of a personal application in the publicity you may give of my lectures; but I shall be very grateful to appear in the public prints as plain *"Elihu Burritt, of Worcester, Mass, who will deliver*

[22] S. D. Hastings (1816-1903) was a reformer, and one of the founders of the Liberty party in Pennsylvania.

a lecture upon LABOR: *on next Tuesday evening March 4th, at —— Hall"*.

I hope to be able to spend about a week in Phila, and promise myself a rich treat in seeing you and friend Cleveland.

Yours cordially—Elihu Burritt

OBERLIN COLLEGE MSS.

CHAPTER II

THE CRUSADE FOR WORLD PEACE

IT was by accident that Burritt's attention was at first
turned toward the crusade against war. This cause
had been upheld by many idealists in Burritt's neigh-
boring town of Hartford, but he had not heard of it. In
fact, the names of such pioneers of peace as Noah Worcester and William Ladd were unknown to him.[1] He
discovered the absurdity of war in the course of preparing a lecture on the anatomy of the earth. Struck by the
arrangements of nature for producing different climates,
soils and products even within the same parallels of lati-
tude, Burritt was compelled to see in the interdepen-
dency of the parts of the earth an argument against war.
Then and there he abandoned the lecture he had planned
and instead wrote one in behalf of peace. When he delivered this lecture at Tremont Theatre in Boston he was
at once enlisted in their cause by the friends of peace. For
the remainder of his life he devoted his major efforts to
the fight against war.

On returning to Worcester Burritt started a weekly
newspaper, *The Christian Citizen*, devoted to temperance, antislavery and world peace. From 1844 until
1851 this paper was continued. Never financially successful, in the end it actually impoverished Burritt. But
its failure and Burritt's poverty did not keep him from
embarking on other journalistic ventures. *The Bond of
Universal Brotherhood*, begun at Worcester in 1846 and

[1] Merle Curti, *The American Peace Crusade, 1815-1860* (Durham, N. C.,
1929), chaps. i and ii.

28

edited in England by both Burritt and Edmund Fry until 1856, was a lively sheet which served as the organ for the League of Universal Brotherhood, an organization founded by Burritt in 1846 and promoted by him in England and on the Continent as well as in America. In these periodicals, in *The Citizen of the World,* and in the *Olive Leaves,* which Burritt also edited, his social philosophy was brought to the attention of thousands of men, women and children. All that Burritt wrote was directed to the plain people, the common man.

In 1846 the conflict between Great Britain and the United States over the Oregon Country threatened war. Burritt, who was editing the *Advocate of Peace and Universal Brotherhood,* the organ of the American Peace Society, determined to spare no efforts to prevent such an outcome. Convinced that only a mass movement in which opinion in the two countries was mobilized and in which pressure was exerted on the governments could be effective, Burritt proceeded to organize what he called "people's diplomacy." Leaflets, picturesquely gotten up and called *Olive Leaves,* were sent out fortnightly to some 1500 American newspapers, scattered in trains, railway stations and other public places and circulated in every other conceivable way. These leaflets or *Olive Leaves* contained convincing statistics regarding the cost of war to the common man, striking anecdotes illustrating the absurdity of an appeal to the sword, and quotations expressing pacific sentiments on the part of well-known English leaders.

The *Olive Leaves* also urged labor groups, as well as merchants, to draw up "friendly addresses" to similar groups in England. American cities with place names identical with the names of English cities, or with industries similar to those of British towns, were urged to make friendly addresses to such towns and cities across the Atlantic. Meanwhile, English friends of peace organized "friendly addresses" to American towns, merchants and workers, some of which bore an impressive number of signatures.

The most interesting address was that from the National Association for Promoting the Political and Social Improvement of the Poor. Written two years before the Communist Manifesto, this address appealed to the class consciousness of working-class comrades in America, urging them not to be seduced into a war to enrich the aristocracy, "our enemies and yours." This remarkable address went on to say that the war spirit had already led the rulers of Great Britain to add to the burdens of labor by increasing the length of militia service. Burritt was much impressed by this address, and remarked that "peace and bread" were associated in the minds of British laborers as intimately as they were in nature.[2]

Thanks to the energy of British Friends, and to the efforts of such men as Cobden, Bright, Douglas Jerrold and Charles Dickens, the "friendly addresses" from America received wide publicity in the British press. And similar addresses from England were extensively noticed in American newspapers. Burritt himself presented an address from Edinburgh to Washington, D. C., unrolling it first before a large group of senators. Among them was John C. Calhoun, one of the most important critics of the war fever. While it would be too much to say that war was prevented by this mobilization

[2] *Christian Citizen*, March 28, 1846; *Advocate of Peace and Brotherhood*, Feb., 1846, p. 56; October, 1846, p. 236; March, 1846, p. 69.

of mass opinion, the "friendly addresses" doubtless facilitated compromise and inspired a much more amicable feeling between the humble people of the two countries.

With penetration and irony Burritt denounced the imperialist movement of Southern slaveowners, holders of Texas script, and land promoters for a war against Mexico. When the war actually came, he uncompromisingly opposed it.

Meanwhile, however, he had gone to Great Britain. After visiting the areas of Ireland most severely afflicted by the famine, Burritt addressed a stirring appeal to his fellow countrymen, urging them to send at once a shipload of provisions to the distressed victims. The Boston Relief Committee responded, and R. B. Forbes, a merchant, volunteered his services as commander of the ship *Jamestown,* which was sent to Cork. The Committee thanked Burritt for his timely appeal.[3]

But it was clear to Burritt that all such humanitarian causes could be best promoted by a permanent, international organization. It was at Pershore, a country village, that he formed, in July, 1846, the League of Universal Brotherhood, devoted to the "elevation of man, as a being, as a brother, irrespective of his country, color, character, or condition." Its members pledged themselves never to enlist in any army or navy, or to yield any voluntary support or sanction to the preparation for or prosecution of any war, by whomsoever, for whatsoever proposed, declared, or waged. The League was open to

[3] See Charles Northend, *Life and Labors of Elihu Burritt, A Memorial Volume* (N. Y., 1879), pp. 225-234, for Burritt's description of the effects of the famine. See also Elihu Burritt, *A Journal of a Visit of Three Days to Skibbereen* (London, 1847); *New York Tribune,* Dec. 31, 1846; and Sarah Forbes Hughes, *Letters and Recollections of John Murray Forbes* (2 vols., Boston, 1899), Vol. I, pp. 120-121.

all men, of whatever country, condition or color, who were willing to take this pledge and to work together for the abolition of all institutions and customs that did not recognize the image of God and a human brother in every man of whatever clime, color or condition. By 1850 twenty-five thousand Americans, and as many British, had signed the pledge, and the work had been extended to Holland and Germany. For the most part the members of the League were humble artisans, workers and farmers, although it included well-known philanthropists and humanitarians. In 1847 and in 1852, when war between England and France seemed imminent, the League sponsored an exchange of "friendly addresses" between English and French towns: 25,000 persons signed the address from Manchester to Marseilles, 1700 signed that from Bordeaux to Birmingham. These addresses disclaimed all sympathy with the harsh sentiments expressed in a large section of the British press, conveyed hearty assurances of esteem and good-will, and invited earnest popular co-operation in strengthening friendly relations between the two countries. Burritt himself carried the addresses from England to twenty-five French cities. Three-fourths of the newspapers of France, Burritt declared, noticed the addresses by printing them or by commenting on them. Burritt believed that "no petition from Parliament, or other document, ever went forth from it, clothed with more moral power" than did the addresses of this popular movement.[4]

Burritt also enlisted the support of the League to carry out an antiwar campaign among the working classes. In 1849 short tracts in French—more "Olive

---

[4] *Addresses amicales du Peuple Anglais au Peuple Français avec un appendice sur un congrès des nations* (Paris, 1848).

Leaves"—were circulated among the workingmen of Paris. When a new decree interfered with this campaign, Burritt got peace propaganda inserted, as concealed advertisements, into the newspapers. *L'Evénement,* a cheap and widely circulated journal, carried such propaganda monthly, and within six months arrangements had been made for the monthly publication of "Olive Leaves" in prominent newspapers in Hamburg, Bremen, Berlin, Stuttgart, Cologne, Frankfort, Copenhagen and St. Petersburg. Before the campaign was brought to an end by the Crimean War and by Burritt's return to America, forty newspapers in seven languages were printing Olive Leaves. The cost of this work was met by contributions from members of the League, by popular bazaars, and by the devoted efforts of "sewing circles." Burritt always regarded this work, which he personally inspired and largely carried out himself, as the happiest experience in his life. There is much evidence that the antiwar arguments in the Olive Leaves reached large numbers of people. Burritt thought that at least 100,000 German soldiers read one of these trenchant criticisms of war each month in a German paper.[5] The Cologne *Gazette* was, in fact, fined for inserting an antiwar argument which the censor regarded as too radical.

Although Burritt counted on and won much support from humanitarians among the substantial middle classes, he realized, far more than his colleagues in the peace movement, the necessity of enlisting the working classes in the antiwar movement. Many workers came out to hear "the learned blacksmith," and Burritt took occasion to point out the financial burdens labor suffered as a re-

[5] *Bond of Brotherhood,* new series, no. 43, Feb., 1854.

sult of militarism and navalism. The unrestrained enthusiasm that greeted him after he had made such addresses to working-class audiences encouraged him to
seize every opportunity to promote the cause of universal peace among the British laborers. His sympathies
seem to have been with the Chartists, and after 1848 he
devoted much time to enlisting support for the antiwar
movement from the working classes in Bethnal Green.

In many respects, however, Burritt's attitude toward
labor was not that of a thoroughgoing radical. He talked
in sentimental and romantic terms of the dignity of labor
and of the beauty of its creative aspects.[6] In this his attitude resembled somewhat that of Carlyle and Ruskin.
His own experience, of course, was that of an artisan,
rather than a factory worker, and he does not seem to
have thoroughly grasped the implications of the indus-
trial revolution. Moreover, his humanitarianism and his
devotion to the Christian principle of love of one's enemies led him to welcome, and to overrate, tendencies of
certain members of the employing class to make conces-
sions to their workers. He looked with favor on the idea
that joint-stock companies might be formed by labor and
capital, in which both would be put in the "same boat,
each with his oar pulling with even beat for the same
shore."[7]

Since Burritt's position was far from being revolutionary, it is the more remarkable that he entertained
some of the ideas that he did. He had no illusions about
the claims of the moneyed aristocracy to superiority, and
he urged workers and farmers not to think of themselves
as an inferior class. "Dont take off your hat in obse-

---

[6] Elihu Burritt, *On the Divine Philosophy of Labor*, MS. Lecture.
[7] *The Bond of Brotherhood*, new series, no. V, May, 1867.

quious reverence to the Girards, Astors, or any speculat-
ing capitalists of the country. Who were they, or who
are the men that have succeeded them, in the ranks of
wealth? they are the oligarcy, are they, that own all the
banks, warehouses, factories, and shipping of the nation?
Grant that. But why should this show of wealth impress
you with a sense of inferiority as a class?" [8] He observed
with some pain that "as America grows richer, the number of poor people in its cities will increase, and their
poverty will become more and more pinching." [9]

Burritt, moreover, vehemently protested against the
wretched exploitation of workers.[10] In Douglas Jerrold's *Weekly Newspaper* he cried out bitterly against
the exploitation of children and in a poignant story
brought home to his readers the frightfulness of this aspect of profit-making. No one more roundly condemned
the existing order for depriving the masses of workers
of the cultivation of mind and spirit, and for flagrant-
ly and continuously violating the doctrine of the brotherhood of man.

Burritt, furthermore, spoke out freely in behalf of so-
cialism. Within an hour from London, he pointed out,
were unused lands which, with proper fertilization,
might be converted into productive farms for the unem-
ployed and impoverished classes. If the state could own
and operate picture galleries, there was no reason why
it might not own and operate such farms.[11] On observing
the manufacture and storage of naval provisions at the
Dockyards and Victualizing Yards at Plymouth, he de-

[8] "The Dignity and Comfort of the Farmer's Life" in Northend, *op. cit*, p.
304.
[9] *Ten Minute Talks on All Sorts of Topics* (London, 1874), p. 246.
[10] Elihu Burritt, *A Walk from London to Land's End* (London, 1865).
[11] *Ibid*, p. 234.

clared that here was proof that "government can run the machine of competitive industry neck and neck with private enterprise." [12] In view of these concrete positions his somewhat florid declaration that, in the New World, at least, labor must be made the heir of all the possibilities and dignities of human life, that there, in any case, it must be the only potentate to be crowned, had substance behind it and was more than a mere generous sentiment.[13]

But it was in the realistic and even revolutionary positon which Elihu Burritt took toward a workingman's movement against war that his vision was most farseeing and his temper most militant. In 1847 he first published *A Way-Word to the Working Men of Christendom.*" It was signed "By a Workingman of America." The pamphlet began by quoting the London *Times* to the effect that nine-tenths of the revenue of the British government came, directly or indirectly, from the working class; that nine-tenths of the national debt which was chiefly the result of war, was owed by the workingmen as much as if they had given their note of hand for it. The pamphlet ended with an eloquent appeal to American workingmen to stand together against war by electing to high office men who could be counted on to keep peace. "Working men of the United States! voters of a young republic! What example will you set at the polls to the hardworking myriads of your brethren in the Old World who lack your right of suffrage to enthrone the sanguinary monster, War! Shall your great officers of the nation 'be peace, and your exactors, righteousness? or shall garments rolled in blood, and fiendish feats of hu-

[12] Elihu Burritt, *A Walk from London to Land's End*, p. 263.
[13] Elihu Burritt, *On the Divine Philosophy of Labor.*

man butchery, qualify your candidate for the highest honor within the nation's gift?" [14]

It is not clear from the records at command when Burritt first advocated a working-man's strike against war. Certainly by 1850 he was trying to insert in the German press appeals to workers to resort to the strike as an instrument for preventing war. Years later, after the First International had been organized, Burritt enthusiastically hailed the antiwar position of workers as one of the most effective means for preventing a great evil. "We hope," he declared in 1867, "the day will come when the working-men of Christendom will form one vast Trades Union, and make a universal and simultaneous *strike* against the whole war system.[15]

And the year following, when the International Congress of Workingmen at Brussels advised a universal strike against war, Burritt wrote, "All hail to this new banner lifted among those millions! It must soon bring the Governments of the world to a better adjudication of their disputes than arbitrament by the sword." [16]

In spite of Burritt's realization of the importance of labor in war, he resembled middle-class pacifists of his time in putting great emphasis on propaganda to push governments into some kind of international organization and juridical machinery for settling conflicts. When the learned blacksmith identified himself with the peace cause in 1843, the project of William Ladd [17] for a court and congress of nations appealed to him as the

[14] Reprinted in *Herald of Peace*, no. lxxxiii (May, 1857), pp. 202-203.
[15] *The Bond of Brotherhood*, new series, no. V, May 1, 1867, pp. 78-79.
[16] *Fireside Words*, Vol. I, no. 10, Oct., 1868, p. 159.
[17] William Ladd, *Essay on a Congress of Nations, for the Adjustment of International Disputes, and for the promotion of universal peace without resort to arms* (Boston, 1840); John Hemmenway, *Memoir of William Ladd, Apostle of Peace* (Boston, 1877), *passim*.

most practical plan the peace movement had favored. English and Continental friends of peace were less enthusiastic than American pacifists for an international juridical organization, and Burritt met with much indifference and opposition.

Undaunted, he determined to promote a popular peace congress in Paris in the midst of the Revolution of 1848, to obtain a hearing for the idea of an international organization of nations to prevent war. The peoples of Europe, aroused and sympathetic with each other, were at the same time in danger of being led into, or of drifting into, a general war. Burritt believed that friends of peace should exert every effort to prevent such a calamity.

Ill, weary, and desperately poor, Burritt arrived in Paris in August, 1848: Liberty poles in the squares and the recently barricaded boulevards bore witness to the revolution. It was, in Burritt's judgment, advisable to organize a popular peace demonstration on as wide a base as possible, and he therefore sought to obtain the help of liberals such as Frédéric Bastiat, Francisque Bouvet, Michel Chevalier, George Sand, Victor Hugo and Horace Say, as well as that of the radicals. But it was impossible to persuade groups with such conflicting ideas to agree on a program for the proposed popular peace congress. *La Démocratie Pacifique* insisted on a commitment to "communism" before giving any aid; and thoroughgoing revolutionists in general feared that such a peace demonstration would, by discouraging the movement for intervention in Italy to aid the revolutionists there, play into the hands of the reactionaries. Moreover, the minister of the interior seemed unwilling either to give or to refuse permission to hold the demonstration.

It was finally decided to hold the peace congress in Brussels, where considerable support from officials was obtained.

On September 20, 1848, the second Popular International Peace Congress opened its sessions in the capital of Belgium.[18] Some hundred and fifty English delegates attended, including the popular orator, Henry Vincent. Resolutions were adopted favoring the general and simultaneous reduction of armaments, a clause in every international treaty stipulating the arbitration of future disputes, a Congress and a Court of Nations, and a more vigorous propaganda against war. Burritt made a spirited address in behalf of a Congress and Court of Nations.[19] Considerable publicity was given the demonstration in the press of both England and the Continent; the resolutions were presented to the governments; and huge and impressive mass meetings were organized and held in the cities of London, Birmingham and Manchester to give additional publicity to the movement. Burritt was chiefly responsible for such measure of success as it had enjoyed.

For the next three years Burritt, whether in Europe or in America, spent the major part of his time and energy in organizing delegations and in arousing enthusiasm for subsequent popular peace congresses. Impressive congresses were held in Paris in 1849, in Frankfort in 1850 and in London in 1851. These were attended by many American, English, French, Dutch and German delegates. For the most part the congresses were supported by liberals, intellectuals and free traders, rather

[18] The first Popular International Peace Congress was held in London in 1843.

[19] Elihu Burritt, "A Congress of Nations," *Old South Leaflets*, no 146 (Boston, n.d.).

than by the working class and revolutionists. But some of the resolutions adopted recognized the economic causes of war and took fairly radical ground in opposing it: loans and imposts for wars of "aggression" were denounced; militarism was attacked as a needless waste and as destructive of economic well-being; the relations between war and slavery were discussed; and the aggressions of so-called civilized peoples on more backward ones were condemned. Burritt, who had done so much to promote these congresses, was greeted with great enthusiasm when he addressed them. Even wider publicity was obtained for these congresses than for that which had inaugurated the series.[20] While the London *Times* ridiculed Burritt and his colleagues, the more liberal journals were sympathetic.[21]

During the Frankfort Congress a request came from the Constitutionalists of Schleswig-Holstein for an investigation of their controversy with Denmark. For the moment there was a truce between the two belligerents. An unofficial commission, made up of Joseph Sturge, the distinguished English Quaker philanthropist, Frederick Wheeler, of Rochester, England, and Elihu Burritt undertook this difficult task. For three months Burritt attempted to induce the authorities in Copenhagen to accept a proposal for arbitration which the provisional government of the duchies had desired to bring to the attention of the Danish government. Burritt's *Journal* contains the complete correspondence between the peace mission and the two governments. Although Austria closed the affair by marching forcibly into the duchies, the value of Burritt's efforts to effect a peaceable adjust-

---

[20] For a description of the congresses, see Curti, *op. cit.*, chap. viii.
[21] London *Times,* Dec. 13, 1848.

ment of the controversy brought praise from the officials of both Schleswig-Holstein and Denmark.[22] Burritt was, nevertheless, glad that he had not shrunk from the trying task of endeavoring to translate his peace principles into action, and took some satisfaction in thinking that it was better to have tried and failed, than not to have tried at all.

Indeed, Burritt, far from being discouraged at the failure of his efforts to prevent war over the Schleswig-Holstein affair, again tried his hand in the diplomatic field in 1853. The Crimean War was imminent, and "the learned blacksmith" tried hard to persuade the American minister to England, Joseph Reed Ingersoll, to offer the mediation of his government to the prospective belligerents. In Washington Burritt enlisted the support of Sumner in behalf of American mediation, and his account of his visit to the White House, and of President Pierce's attitude toward the suggestion, is very interesting. The whole episode throws considerable new light on the movement for pushing the United States actively forward on the international stage.

Although Burritt's efforts to prevent the Crimean War failed, one cannot withhold admiration for his courageous and intelligent activities as a friend of international peace. No student of the history of propaganda can afford to overlook his descriptions of his manifold efforts to counteract the martial spirit.

[22] Curti, *op. cit.*, pp. 183-186; Reedtz to Burritt, Copenhagen, Oct. 29, 1850, no. 142, *Aar 1850, Departemental inne politisk Brevvexling*, Rigsarkiv, Copenhagen.

[MS. JOURNALS]

[Worcester] Wednesday, Jan 1st 1845

I have entered upon another year, and may He whose long-suffering compassion has borne with me so long, prepare me for what it may be my lot to suffer and do, and be during the coming year, if I am permitted to see it close. I have laid out a good deal of work in the cause of humanity, which I hope I may have strength to perform. I find my mind is setting with all its sympathies toward the subject of Peace. I am persuaded that it is reserved to crown the destiny of America, that she shall be the great peace maker in the brotherhood of nations. And I think that I cannot better employ the talents and time that God may give me, than to devote a year or two to this cause. I have therefore conceived a design of making a tour through the Western Country this winter, with the view of presenting the principles and objects of Peace. . . .

Friday [January] 31 [1845]

Commenced drawing a diagram of the plan for our peace operations. Worked with a good deal of enthusiasm until noon. Friends Walker [23] & Coues [24] came in to attend the conference in the evening. We met at friend Blanchard's [25] and our conference realised my apprehensions. My plan was to embody all the advocates of the peace cause that we could enlist in the enterprise and furnish 26 original articles, each week, for 26 leading papers, one in each state of the Union. I insisted that sending these articles in manuscript, each addressed personally to the editor of a paper

[23] Amasa Walker (1799-1873), political economist, pacifist, abolitionist. Walker was elected to the Massachusetts Senate in 1849, and in 1851 became Secretary of State of Massachusetts.

[24] Samuel C. Coues, of Portsmouth, N. H., was a humanitarian and leader in the American peace movement.

[25] Joshua Blanchard (1782-1868), Boston merchant, abolitionist and radical pacifist.

would secure their admission; whereas if sent in printed slips they would most generally be rejected. Another argument I urged was this, that if sent in manuscript as the communications of individuals residing in different parts of the Union, they would exert more influence upon the public mind than if proceeding from some office in New England. The people would be impressed with the idea that a great change had come over public sentiment, if all at once, the newspapers should begin and continue to speak upon the subject of Peace. Another consideration I presented, was, that the labor to carry on the enterprise would employ every friend of peace with something to do, thus consolidating them all in a great system of action. But all my efforts were in vain. My plan was highly commended, but was deemed too large. One of a boyish expansion was concluded upon, and I went back to the Marlboro chagrined and disheartened at the issue of what I thought to be a magnificent system of effort.

Friday [March] 28 [1845]

Wrote with a good deal of interest an article for my "school-room," in which I appealed to the Boys of the World, who are soon to govern the governments of it, not to pour out their blood and treasure in idolatrous oblations to National flags; summing up the expense of this idolatry to the people of Christian nations. In the afternoon I called upon Isaac Davis who endorsed the note I obtained of Pratt with great readiness, which gave me much pleasure. My money matters are becoming very close, and the prospect looks gloomy in its pecuniary aspects. My paper does not yet pay its own expenses, and I have long ago spent the little pittance I had saved. I have nothing before me but a determination to give my life to the cause of humanity, and the hope that humanity will give me in return my victuals and clothes. I leave it with Providence, which has thus far brought me safely on my way.

Bristol [England] Oct 9 1846

[To James Clark [26]]

Dear Friend Clark

I was right glad to get your letter of the 29th. I am much better than when I left you, although I have been on the *qui vive* continually. Had a grand time in Exeter— nearly 1200 were present on last Friday evening, when the Address from the women of Phila. was presented. I delivered my new peace lecture and its radical principles were received much better than I expected. Several speeches were made and it was a stirring occasion. Owing to excitement on the evening before the lecture, I was suffering a severe sick or nervous headache when I arose to address such a large audience. I forgot it under the pressure of my effort, but it came upon me like a giant refreshed with new vim after I had finished, and I had a tough time of it in the night. Recovered next day so as to sit for my portrait to two artists. In the evening met a circle at R. W. Fox's, and laid before them the plan of the League, and several signed. On Monday I delivered a lecture before the Litany Society and had a good audience. Stopt an hour at Bridgewater and saw Thompson. They have secured about 30 signatures. Last night we had a grand meeting in Broad Mead, Bristol. Samuel Browley was present, and was exceedingly happy. I spoke about 1 ¼ hours. They are going ahead here in the League wonderfully and have obtained nearly 300 names already. I think Bristol bids fair to be the centre of the movement. Everything looks auspicious. I leave for Gloucester on Saturday, where I am to lecture on Sunday evening. I left the articles you speak of intentionally, as they are worn out,—perhaps some poor person might wear the pantaloons some longer. I saw Sally in Exeter on Mon-

[26] James Clark (1811-1906) was a Quaker leather manufacturer of Street, Somerset. He was interested in peace, temperance and other philanthropic movements in labors for which he was closely associated with his cousin, Joseph Sturge.

day evening. I shall send more than 200 names by this
steamer. Shall be in Birmingham on Monday or Tuesday.
Anything to the care of Joseph Sturge will reach me.

Ever yours

Elihu Burritt

Please remember me to your wife and all the members of
both families

MS. COLLECTIONS
Friends House Library

Manchester Feb 6 [18]47

Dear Friend Clark

I am on the eve of leaving for Ireland, to fathom the
cause, extent & cure of its misery. I know not what may
befall me there—but I shall hope for the best. I am greatly
mortified that the Citizens have not come regularly to you.
I have written to Ezekiel about it, and hope it will be soon
rectified. I hope you will regard the League movement as
a practical system of philanthropy, as an active society.
Can you not get up a meeting occasionally of its members
in Street, and assure more and more a fixed and efficient
organization? Do not let it die out for want of interest.
The League branch in Bridgewater is already dead from
that cause. Could not your nephew there find some young
man who is not enslaved to mammon, who would act as secretary, and try to resuscitate the few to life? Please address
me in Birmingham, as before.

Ever Yours

Elihu Burritt

MS. COLLECTIONS
Friends House Library

[MS. JOURNALS]

[London] Monday, July 19 [1847]

Wrote with all my might until the American mail closed
at 6 P.M. Gave a description of our League Meeting in

London. Wrote a short article declining my nomination as a candidate for the Vice Presidency of the United States by a new Liberty Party recently formed in New York upon a Free Trade basis as well as Anti-slavery. Directed Drew [27] to see and sound young Bartlett [28] in reference to his coming over to France as my assistant.

Wednesday, July 21 [1847]

Wrote rather a long article for the Bond, under the heading "*A Wayword to the Workingmen of Christendom, by a Workingman of America.*" I intend to have it printed on an Olive Leaf and distributed by itself in the large manufactories of the Kingdom. I think I shall follow it up with several on the subject of war, to be scattered more broadcast than the Bond can do.

Bristol Aug 20 [1847?]

[To James Clark]

Dear Friend

I can write but a moment now, as I am much exhausted, owing to the excitement and labor I have endured for some days past. I rejoice that you are doing such a good work for the League. I shall consider you one of my right hand co-partners in this glorious enterprise. I received the list of names you sent with great pleasure. I have just sent 160 names to America to be hung out there under the Pledge & will write as soon as I get a little rested to Fathers Martin & Matthew. Have you plenty of Pledges? Hope you will have a good supply on hand always, so as to leave a few on the way to be filled at the solicitations of those you may interest in the movement. Hope you will also have a few "Bonds" to show or give as specimens. Any person can obtain a packet of 100 through the post by remitting 3/6 in postage stamps to J. Showell, Birmingham (see note at the

---

[27] Thomas Drew, publisher of the *Christian Citizen* at Worcester, Massachusetts.

[28] David Bartlett acted as Burritt's assistant in London for a year.

end of the Bond) I shall be in Bristol until the 25th. Shall be glad to hear from you & receive what names you may have procured. I am meeting little social circles for the purpose of introducing the League at Gloucester, 24 signed, at Bristol last night 27. So you see I may be able to pick up many in this way. . . .

Truly yours,
Elihu Burritt

MS. COLLECTIONS
Friends House Library

[MS. JOURNALS]

[Paris] Monday, Sept. 13. [1847]

Arose early, and wrote until 11, when I called upon Mr. Doherty, editor of the Democratic Pacifique, who received me with great cordiality. He has already published my Memoirs from the People's Journal, and thus introduced me to his readers with a notice of the League movement. He offered to insert articles on Peace, Free Trade, &c, provided they were written so as to conform with the genius of his paper, which is the organ of Fourierism. He said the French had been mocked [?] so long by the Roman Catholic religion, that they dislike any thing that savours of theological phraseology. This, perhaps, is the secret of their infidelity. He introduced me to several of the *virtuosos* of the Fourier Phalanx, solemn looking visionary spirits who could not speak English, and as I could not speak French, it was difficult to get into much conversation. I think I shall not try to get anything into their organ, as it is in questionable reputation for its moral character. I returned to my lodgings and wrote the remainder of the day for the Citoyen. Murray called in the evening, and we had another conversation on the subject of his acting as a correspondent for the League. I think I will entrust him with the mere business department of the work. After he left I had a long earnest discussion with an English official on the republican system of government.

[Brussels] Sept. Thursday, 16 [1847]

Arose with one of my nervous headaches owing to reading too long last evening. Went to the bureau of the Committee of the Free Trade Association, and gave them my credentials as delegate from Oberlin, Ohio, and received a Card of Membership & ticket of Admission. Went to the Hotel de Ville, where the Convention was to hold its sessions, and found 100 or more of the delegates already assembled. In the course of an hour, the room was well filled by the most interesting audience I ever saw. There were men from most all the continental nations, grave, thoughtful, moustachioed men, some with foreheads ridged with the sallowest German wrinkles; young men with sickly age in their faces, as if the sleepless energy of their thoughts had eaten out all the vivacity of youth. A serious, middle aged man took the chair, and made an introductory speech with grave emphasis, adverting to the objects of the Convention. The meeting was then organized and several officers appointed; after which the discussions were open & conducted with much spirit until 4 P.M. Dr Bowring,[29] Mr Ewart,[30] & Col Thompson [31] from England made short but eloquent speeches in French, in which they uttered noble sentiments of universal brotherhood. To me this meeting was one of the deepest interest, as much as if it were one emanating from the League of Universal Brotherhood. The principles discussed were all within the compass of our constitution, and all the result of them will accrue to our cause—to the pro-

[29] Sir John Bowring (1792-1872), linguist, traveler, friend and adviser of Jeremy Bentham, member of Parliament, British consul at Canton.

[30] William Ewart (1798-1869), liberal politician, reformer and member of Parliament.

[31] Thomas P. Thompson (1783-1867), utilitarian philosopher, politician, editor of the *Westminster Review*.

motion of good will & fraternal intercourse among men. Owing to my headache I did not go to the banquet prepared for the members of the Convention by the Brussels Free Trade Association, which has provided the most liberal entertainments for the delegates.

London, Saturday, Jan 1 1848.

A New Year has come, 1848! Thanks be to the Great Father of all that I am permitted to see the opening of this new period of time. Thanks to his name for all the mercies that have surrounded me during the past year; they have been new every morning, noon and night. It has been a hard year of labour, of much anxiety but of great mercy. The League, too, has grown and taken root beyond all my expectations. At the commencement of the last year, it numbered about 10,000, now nearly 40,000, and the good and true have come into it, on both sides of the Atlantic. What will be my condition when another New Year shall dawn upon the world? . . . . Wrote a few letters, and sent to newspapers in the West Indies copies of the Wesleyan containing a full report of our Bristol Meeting. In the evening, several of the League Brethren came in, and we had a long conference upon getting up a Friendly Address from London to the inhabitants of Paris signed by 500,000 persons. We resolved to try the experiment.

[Manchester] Wednesday Feb. 23 [1848]

Went with George Bradshaw[32] to Bolton, to visit Mr Bazely's great cotton factory. Mr B. took us over his extensive establishment which is conducted in a truly admirable way. We visited all his schools for the children of the operatives, and at 12 about 500 persons employed in the mills assembled in his great lecture room and I made a short speech to them. Leaving this establishment we proceeded to that of Henry Holdsworth, which is distinguished by the

[32] George Bradshaw (1801-1853), originator of railway guides, English Quaker, philanthropist.

largest water wheel 63 feet in diameter. Took tea with Mr H. where we met a large circle of his friends. Returned to Manchester about 7; and found Crosfield [33] & Mussey at Conningham's making preparations for the meeting of the ensuing evening. They had drawn up an excellent Address to Lyons. After Mussey had left, we talked over some long plans of operations connected with the League movement. I proposed that a great meeting should be held in May, not only for the English Branch, but also for the Universal League; also a deputation to Paris of Leaguers from England to commune with our French brethren.

[Paris] Friday, April 7 [1848]

. . . . After reading and writing a little, I walked out to see the Revolutionary City and its men in blouse. Was surprised to find all so quiet. There was a placidity and thoughtful humour in the faces of the people. I walked all the afternoon, following the Boulevards to their whole extent and through narrow and obscure streets, and I never heard or saw anything of a violent nature. I purposely mingled with the redoutable men in blouse, and found them generally serious, well looking and tolerably well clad, with active life and speculation in their eyes, and quite the reverse of the dull, pale, dirty masses which one meets in London.

The posture of affairs in Great Britain is at the crisis-point, and attracts the attention and solicitude of the thoughtful. Between the Repealers and the Chartists, the country is verging toward a struggle the like of which it has not witnessed for a century . . . The petition for the People's Charter is said to present an army of 5,000,000 signatures! . . . It is pretty evident that one result of these popular agitations and overturnings of old dynasties will be a reconstruction of nationalities in Europe, accord-

[33] Joseph Crosfield, English Friend who, with Burritt, was responsible for the exchange of Friendly Addresses between England and the United States in 1846.

ing to social, religious and political affinities. At least it may be predicated that all who speak the same language on the Continent will resolve themselves into one nation. Thus the Continental People will be relieved of the burden of several independent establishments.

Saturday, April 8 [1848]

. . . . Painful anxiety is felt in reference to the result of the Chartist meeting and procession in London on Monday next. It is rumoured here that many propagandists have left Paris for that metropolis, in order to stimulate agitation or bias popular movements. It is stated that ten thousand regular troops will be under arms on Monday, prepared for any extremities. . . A few days will, it is feared, leave the record of sad events upon a new page of English history. God grant that no syllables of that experience be written in blood.

Saturday, April 15 [1848]

Wrote till 2 P.M., when Mr Hawke and several French & Italian gentlemen called, and we had a long and animated conference upon the subject of the convention in Paris and a Congress of Nations. They all promised to do all in their power to prepare for the Convention, and to get the idea before the public through the press. I found that they were "Communists,[34] but willing to waive their one idea" for the discussion of some practical measure for establishing peace. . . . .

Sunday, April 16 [1848]

. . . Mr Hawke called at 4, and I went with him to call upon a Mr Cabet [?]. We found the city in almost a revolutionary state. The quais on both sides of the Seine from the Tuileries as far as the eye could search were crowded by the National Guards, nearly 100,000 of whom were out, marching through the city, singing the Marseillaise and

---

[34] Burritt is referring to the Utopian Socialists.

crying "A bas la Communistes! Vive La Republique," &c.
This demonstration was called out to oppose one of the multitude directed against the government. It appears that the
Communists are inciting the people on to demand and
procure a division of property, or a general confiscation
in favour of the multitude; and that this military manifestation was to overawe them. Never did I witness such a
scene. The Marseillaise was sung by thousands of the National Guards as they marched with their glittering bayonets through the city. It was the last sound I heard when
I had retired to rest.

Monday, April 17 [1848]

. . . . At 11 several gentlemen called most of whom
were Communists. Two of them were from Portugal. We
had a long discussion of the subject of a Congress of Nations. One of them was so vehemently in favour of putting
the principle of the Socialists before any other, for the
purposes of establishing peace that no definite result was
attained, though all approved the plan I proposed. . . .
My time is nearly exhausted, and I shall not be able to see
many more persons while in Paris. . . .

[London] Monday, October 30th, 1848

. . . At 1 P.M. we repaired to the official residence of the
Premier.[35] It was a new position to find myself in, and my
mind was running back over the road by which I had been
led from my youth up to this interview with the Prime
Minister of England. Surely I have daily reasons to humble
myself before God in grateful adoration for all his loving
kindness. We were ushered into a waiting room, where we
remained for a few minutes; then were shown into the presence of Lord John Russell. I could hardly realize that the
little, thin, wrinkled, premature old man who rose from
behind a common counting room table was the Atlas upon

---

[35] Lord John Russell (1792-1878).

whom the British Empire rested. He received us with a politeness that seemed to be an unbending of aristocracy. Wm. Ewart in a rather confused and embarrassed manner, introduced us, whereupon M. Visschers [36] prefaced the reading of the Address with a few remarks, then commenced the document in a slow and impressive manner. Lord John held a copy of the Address in his hands, and followed Mr Visschers as he read. I glanced at his countenance occasionally, and saw it assume different expressions as he listened to the principles and arguments which we had addressed to governments, as the voice of the Congress. Sometimes there was a kind of incredulous pursing up of his lips, as if he would say "this is all very well, but it won't do." Occasionally he would dart a sharp look at the reader, disclosing the white of his eyes, like heat lightning glancing across a summer cloud. After the reading was finished, Wm. Ewart gave a brief description of the composition of the Brussels Congress, and was followed with a few remarks by Mr Scoble and Richards. I then spoke for a few minutes, stating that the peace principles had taken a deep hold of the popular mind in the United States, notwithstanding the unfortunate war with Mexico; that the friends of peace were active in propagating their principles, infusing them into the education of the young, &c. I alluded to the efforts which had been put forth to sow and cultivate the seeds of good-will between the people of the United States and the mother country. I closed by referring to the fact, that in the recent treaty with Mexico, it was stipulated that all questions of difficulty henceforth arising between the two nations, should be submitted to arbitration.[37] When he had

[36] Auguste Visschers (1804-1874), Belgian publicist and liberal.

[37] This was the first instance in modern times in which such a provision was inserted in an international treaty. For the interesting way in which it was done see M. E. Curti. "Pacifist Propaganda and the Treaty of Guadelupe Hidalgo," *American Historical Review*, Vol. XXXIII (Apr., 1928), pp 596-598.

concluded, Lord John commenced his reply in a courteous spirit, taking up our different propositions *seriatim*. He mentioned some of the difficulties in the way of realising either of the measures embodied in our Resolutions, without disclosing his opinion fully in regard to their ultimate practicability. He said that he did not doubt that such meetings as the Brussels Congress would tend to exercise a salutary influence upon Governments, and induce a spirit of moderation and concession, should questions of difference or difficulty arise between them. He admitted that the military establishments of Europe were extensive and costly, especially those of continental nations. He thought England had evinced a spirit not only to live at peace, but to promote peace between nations; that her armament was not large compared with that of other powers. He admitted that the minister or heads of a Government who hurried a people into war, incurred a fearful responsibility. He addressed more remarks to me than I had expected. He said he was glad to hear the statements I had made in reference to progress of the peace principles among the people of the United States, and to the prevalence of a friendly feeling towards the Mother Country. Alluding to the treaty with Mexico, containing the arbitration clause, he said with strong emphasis, that if the United States should think proper to make a similar proposal to the British Government, it would be taken into their most serious consideration. This was an important admission, for it conceded the principle of arbitration completely; as the British Government would stand pledged to enter into the same treaty stipulations with all other nations, which should make the proposal. . . .

15 New Broad Street, London
May 19 1849

Gerrit Smith Esq.[38]
Dear Friend of Humanity,

Permit me to address to you an earnest appeal to attend the approaching Peace Congress in Paris. If there be one man in America above any other, who ought to be present at that august demonstration, *thou art the man*—representing all the Christian philanthropies of America in your own character and labours. We look forward to an Assembly which shall make a profound impression upon the whole civilized world. The great Lamartine, and leading men of the French National Assembly will be there; Cobden, his compere, and many of the enlightened members of the British Parliament will be there; enlightened legislators from Germany, & other continental countries will be there, and hundreds of good men and true from both sides of the English Channel, and of the Atlantic. There you would meet probably 500 or 1000 of the purest men of England, many of whom would greet you as a long-tried brother in works of love and liberty for men of every colour and country.

We are anxious, above expression, that America should be represented by a delegation that might speak the great voice of the New World to the congregated peoples of the Old in the French metropolis. Let me entreat you not to refuse this appeal. Your presence and participation in the Congress would do honour to America, and great service to the cause of universal brotherhood. The Congress of Nations Committee in Boston are organizing to charter a ship

[38] Gerrit Smith (1797-1874) was a lawyer and wealthy landowner of Petersboro, New York. He was most distinguished, however, as a reformer and Ultra-Abolitionist. He was a member of the House of Representatives from 1853-1854. His associations with Burritt were close. See O. B. Frothingham, *Gerrit Smith: A Biography* (N. Y., 1878).

to freight with delegates, and I hope you will head the phalanx of these missionaries of peace.

In the Bonds of Brotherhood,

Ever Yours

Elihu Burritt

BURRITT MSS.

Library of the Institute of New Britain

[MS. JOURNALS]

Monday, June 11 [1849]

. . . The grand *finale* of the one hundred & fifty Public Meetings and of all the other operations which the Peace Congress Committee had instituted during the last six months, in support of Mr Cobden's Motion,[39] was now at hand. The rills of public sentiment which had been threading their way up to St. Stephens through city, town, village and rural communities, from Land's End to John O'Groats, were now to be concentrated upon Parliament in the volume and "the voice of a multitude of mighty waters," pressing it to the august utterance of a nation's voice in favour of Peace and the brotherhood of nations. A thousand petitions, some bearing the signatures of 10,000 individuals each, had conveyed to that body intimations of the people's will. To me, who had never before witnessed a phenomenon or assisted at an experiment of this character, it was deeply interesting to observe the process and effect of this "pressure from without" upon the Central Legislature of the world. The mind-machinery set in operation to produce this pressure, was in itself fraught with instruction to Governments and Peoples. It was the silent enginery of invisible activities concentrating the individual wills of communities upon the minds of statesmen like an impalpable presence of conviction, and turning them to the bias of ideas which they had perhaps ridiculed and resisted.

[39] For the insertion of arbitration clauses in treaties with foreign Powers.

First of the dynamics of this machinery of popular opinion and sentiment, planted "in a little upper room" and opened upon the Legislature of the greatest Empire in the World, was the *Penny Post*. For the six months "agitation" of the national mind which the Peace Congress Committee had originated and conducted in favour of the measure to be brought forward by Mr Cobden,[40] the Penny Post had been plied with unremitting activity. Nearly 50,000 letters, and other missiles, in manuscript or lithograph, had been sent out in every direction like radiating veins of thought through which the "one idea" was kept in lively circulation. Thus, it acquired a constituency of earnest minds in almost every town in the Kingdom which sent a representative to Parliament; and that representative had perhaps been surprised to receive at St. Stephens by the Penny Post communications from his own constituents requesting him, with the emphasis of electors, to give his voice and vote for Mr Cobden's Motion. Then hundreds of thousands of printed leaves elucidating "the one idea" had been scattered with a sower's hand among the masses of the people, which they had read eagerly on their way to the field or factory; and the silent conviction of myriads of men, women & children of the labouring classes, who had no votes to give or withhold, had strengthened the pressure of the people's mind upon Parliament. Then every night, for six months, a public meeting, in some city, town or village, had given an utterance to "the one idea" which the Press echoed and reechoed among the populations far and near. Thus one hundred and fifty assemblies of the people, from John O'Groats to Land's End, embracing the active minds of as many distinct communities, had thrown into the gathering tide of public opinion the force of their sympathies. And the Great Meeting in Exeter Hall was to give a great

[40] Richard Cobden (1804-1865), British statesman, advocate of free trade and international peace. Burritt was on familiar terms with Cobden.

voice to all these sympathies and convictions of the people,
and to speak to Parliament the last word of the nation in
favour of the measure to be discussed in the House of Commons on the ensuing evening. . . . But, in addition to all
these agencies and influences, which had been, or were to
be, brought to bear upon Parliament, to constrain it to
speak a great word of peace to the Struggling nations of
Europe, it was thought of great importance to elicit from
Sir Robert Peel an expression of pacific sentiments which
should give that word additional emphasis. . . The great
statesman, who still wields an influence which is felt through
Europe, received us with the easy courtesy and affable ur-
banity of a natural gentleman . . . . [the Committee] expressing the hope that Sir Robert Peel, even if he could not
support the Motion of Mr Cobden, would avail himself of
the opportunity to give such an expression to his views on
the general subject of Peace . . . The illustrious Baronet
then replied in a tone and manner which evinced his desire to impress us with the conviction of his sympathy
with the spirit and object of all practical measures for the
promotion of peace among the nations. He spoke of the
evils and horrors of war in strong terms of deprecation;
and of the duty of Governments to exhaust all pacific and
honourable means before resorting to arms. He referred
to the pacific policy which England had maintained and
illustrated for a long course of years; to the many instances
in which the British Government had offered its mediation
between contending powers. He admitted that the principle of arbitration might and ought to be adopted in many
cases of international controversy. Still he thought that it
would be necessary to defer a reference to arbitration until
the cases occurred, as it would be impossible to foresee the
circumstances under which they would transpire. He doubted
whether a convention for a settlement by arbitration could
be entered into by Governments indefinitely in advance of
the questions to be adjusted. He alluded to some cases in

which arbitration would not be practicable, and others in which it would be surrounded with difficulties which could only be met when they occurred. We could see that he suggested these objections not as insuperable obstacles to the principle of arbitration, nor in a way to diminish our confidence in its practicability, as an effectual substitute for war, but rather in support of a foregone conclusion that arbitration could not be *organised* into a fixed system, but must be left, as it had been, to the option of the nations involved in a controversy, and to be suited to all the contemporaneous circumstances of the case. . .

[Paris] Sunday, July 15 [1849]

. . . At 11 we repaired to the Hôtel Des Affaires Etrangères, and here were ushered directly into the receiving room of the Minister [de Tocqueville],[41] who entered from the garden in a few minutes. He received us with a pleasant smile and truly French politeness, which made us quite at home with him. After being introduced by Mr Sumner [42] to him, he adverted immediately to the subject of the Congress, and inquired the character of the demonstration. Mr Richard [43] then gave an exposition of the principles and progress of the movement, beginning with the Brussels Congress; alluded to the Minister's pacific sentiments and policy and expressed our hope that he would accord his sympathy to the proposed demonstration.

M. de Tocqueville then replied in French, and thanked us for [what] we had said in commendation of his course and character. In reference to the question of peace, there

[41] Alexis de Tocqueville (1805-1859), French political theorist and statesman, was Minister of Foreign Affairs of the Republic, 1849-1852. He is known in this country for his *Democracy in America*, first published in 1835.

[42] George Sumner was a brother of Charles Sumner and for many years resided in France.

[43] Henry Richard (1812-1888), reformer and parliamentarian, had recently assumed the chief office in the English Peace Society, an office which he held for forty years. Richard and Burritt were closely associated in the work of organizing the Peace Congress at Frankfort in 1850, and in many kindred activities. See Charles S. Miall, *Henry Richard, M. P.* (London, 1889).

was but one voice in France, and that was in its favour.
But with this unanimous desire for peace, there was much
difference and doubt in reference to its realisation by any
plans which had been proposed; and although personally his
sympathies were with all efforts to accomplish such a desirable end he feared that its attainment was far distant.
He had heard of the Congress at Brussels, and cordially
approved of such demonstrations, said that if we did not
meet with such cordial support in France as we might
expect, we must not be disappointed, nor impute it to cold-
ness or indifference to the objects we had in view, but
rather to a want of confidence in the means employed to
attain them. He thought the character of the delegates
would be a guaranty against the introduction into the discussion of extraneous or political topics, or allusions to the
contemporaneous events, which would tend to excite agitation. He dwelt upon this point with some seriousness, in-
quiring what means we proposed to adopt, to prevent persons availing themselves of the opportunity afforded by the
Congress, to broach political and questionable subjects. We
assured him that all who were admitted as members would
be expected to give their full adhesion to the basis of the
Congress, and to be admitted by cards of membership. We
then alluded to the progress of the cause in England, and
to the friendly spirit towards France which pervaded the
English mind. He said he was gratified to hear our statements in reference to the existence of this feeling, as it
corroborated his own convictions. He was glad to say that
the same sentiment was coming to be reciprocated in France;
and that it was incorrect and unjust to suppose that the
French were more disposed to foreign war than any other
people. The peasants were not fond of the military life, but
preferred to remain at home and cultivate their little farms.
That although they fought well as soldiers, and evinced
great animation in a campaign, they nearly all return to
their homes at the expiration of their term of service. He

had observed especially this trait in the African army . . .
In conclusion, he said we should see M Dufaure, the Minister of the Interior, on the next day, and would converse
with him on the subject of the Congress . . .

                                   Utica, Feb 23 1850
[Hon. Gerrit Smith]
My dear Sir.

I have arrived thus far on my trip to Buffalo.[44] I regret
sincerely and deeply that I am not able to call and see you
at Petersboro. Every night is engaged until I return to
Albany. But I enclose you the notice of a Peace Convention at Albany which I hope it may be possible for you to
attend. Can you not be present on this occasion? I hope
and pray that you may be with us. We need your counsel,
countenance and sympathy. Do, please, bend your circumstances and engagements to the possibility of meeting the
friends of peace at that Convention. I expect to be in Lockport on Thursday night next, and should be happy to
receive a line from you at that place.

                         Ever & Truly Yours
                         Elihu Burritt

BURRITT MSS.
Library of the Institute of New Britain

[MS. JOURNALS]

[Berlin] Friday, July 19 [1850]

. . . After dinner we remained in our room, as we expected a call from Prof. Muencker [?]. He came at 7, and
spent 2 hours with us. His mind seemed heavily depressed
in view of the condition of Germany. But the saddest aspect
to him, was the secondary position of Prussia among the

[44] Burritt was making an extensive tour of the Northern and Western
states in behalf of the Peace Congress movement, with the special purpose
of enlisting delegates to the Conference which was held the following summer at Frankfort.

first rate powers; not the loss of or deprivation of individual liberty which the Prussians are suffering from their own Government. As an instance of the despotism which has been exercised, to keep down the public mind, he said an American by the name of Ryder was arrested and tried, and ordered to quit the country for the sin of his *nationality*, and not for a single act or expression which could be questioned. Because he was an American, he was suspected to be a secret emissary propagating democratic ideas among the people. It was sad to see a man thus affected. He seemed like most of the Germans that we have met, to have no faith in anything except brute force. The government had a mighty army of it at their command, and the people could do nothing until they could overpower that force. This seemed to be his idea. We tried to argue with him, showing the impotence of brute force issues either for the people or for Governments . . .

[Copenhagen] Wednesday, Sept. 11 [1850]

. . . We were conducted to the room of the Foreign Minister without any ceremony or delay, and he received us in a simple natural way, inviting us to sit down upon a sofa with him . . . Joseph Sturge introduced the subject of the interview, and asked permission to read to him the statement which he had already sent to Count Moltke, whereupon he replied that the Count had sent him the copy we left with him and that he had read it. Frederic Wheeler and I then addressed to him the same remarks as we had to the other minister in the morning. Mine were substantially these:

"The statement which Mr Sturge has just read to you expresses our united views and convictions in reference to our voluntary mission to the Danish Government. We deemed it due to this important subject that this statement should be reduced to writing, that the public might not misapprehend the object and result of this interview. In asking the Government of Denmark to submit the whole question at issue to the decision of enlightened and impartial arbitration, we do not ask them to peril or forego any of their just rights. We merely ask them to establish those rights before an impartial tribunal, which shall determine them according to the principles of strict justice and equity. And it seems that this very method of adjusting the present difficulty between Denmark and the Duchies has been expressly prescribed by solemn treaty between the two countries. By the terms of this treaty, it appears that the persons who should be appointed to constitute the court of arbitration, were to be released for the time being from their oaths of allegiance in order that they might be in a condition to pronounce an unbiased decision. Although the present state of open war might render it impossible to constitute such a court of persons selected from the two countries, yet we believe that enlightened and impartial men may be found in other nations, who would command the confidence of both parties, and to whom they might safely submit their respective claims. The Government and people of Schleswig-Holstein have declared themselves ready and willing to refer their rights to such a tribunal. All that is now wanting to prevent the further effusion of precious blood, and to establish peace on a satisfactory and permanent basis, is the assent of Denmark to this mode of adjustment, and her co-operation in carrying it into effect. And we would indulge the hope, that a country just entering upon the career of constitutional government and liberal institutions, would be willing to inaugurate its course by such an act of justice and generosity towards a people which it wishes to embrace within its own charter of freedom. The settlement of the existing difference by arbitration, would release Denmark from all those obligations to foreign intervention or diplomacy, which might hereafter obstruct or embarrass the full development of her free institutions; whilst at the same time, it would lay that foundation for a lasting peace and harmony with the Duchies, which could not be secured even by their complete subjugation by the sword. Millions of minds in Germany and other countries are becoming intensely excited on this question; and it is bringing foreign governments into collision with each other, and with their own subjects. We cannot but apprehend the most serious consequences to the general peace of Europe if Denmark should refuse that just mode of settlement which the Duchies have declared themselves willing to accept. If, therefore, the Minister of Foreign Affairs could, on the part of the Danish Govt, say to us, as individuals, what the Duchies have said, we believe that an immediate end might be put to this deplorable war and measures adopted for establishing peace upon an honourable and satisfactory basis, and we would entreat you, by all the solemn responsibilities that attach to persons in your position; by all that is precious in the destiny of the thousands of human beings whose lives may hang upon your response, not to refuse this just mode of settlement which the Duchies are willing to accept."

He listened throughout with serious attention, and when we had concluded our remarks he replied. He said he had served his country for many years, but had retired with a desire to pursue his course as a man of science; but that he had been unexpectedly recalled to office. His greatest desire was peace, and the study of every hour was to effect an amicable settlement with the Duchies. He appreciated our good-will in seeking to predispose the two parties to peace. On his part he had given many guarantees of his desire to put a stop to the war. He had drawn up or signed three Armistices: which had been rejected or broken by the Duchies.

He presented to us copies of the Manifesto signed by the King, and dated July 14, which contained terms of settlement. This had been disregarded or rejected by the Schleswig-Holsteiners. Still they were willing to renew the same offer. It was not the fault of Denmark that the war was begun or continued. He alluded to the London Protocol, as containing a decision in favour of Denmark. We observed that it appeared to be issued at the request of Denmark, and could not be considered as the avowal of arbitration, as Schleswig-Holstein was not consulted in the matter, and was no party to it. He admitted this indirectly. He returned to and dwelt much upon the indisposition of the Duchies to listen to any overtures. Being anxious to bring him to the single point of arbitration, we tried to elicit an answer from him in reference to this mode of settlement. But after some circumlocution, he said he should see his colleagues the next day, and if their opinion was favourable, he would communicate it to us at our hotel. . . . still we did not elicit from him either his assent to or dissent from the principle of arbitration. On our way back we resolved to be plain and write him for a distinct reply in writing which we intended to publish. If we can state to the public that one of the contending parties offered to refer the question in dispute to arbitration and that the other refused such a mode of adjustment, we shall show that our mission has not been without a practical result. We believe that it has exerted a salutary influence already upon both parties. Perhaps it was the first time that they were ever addressed on the subject by any other persons than cold calculating diplomatists. It has demonstrated the practicability of private & disinterested individuals interposing pacific propositions and counsels between two countries even at the most embittered moment.

Hamburgh, Hotel de Bavière, Nov 25 1850
Rev L. S. Jacoby.[45]
My Dear Sir
I have taken the liberty of sending you two or three nos. of my little monthly magazine, *The Bond of Brotherhood,* which I hope you have received and found time to read. If so, you will see the spirit and object of that branch

---

[45] The Rev. Ludwig Jacoby was a pastor residing at Bremen.

of the friends of peace associated in the League of Brotherhood. I hope the principles advocated in the "Bond" which is the organ of this association, are in sympathy with your convictions. I am the President of the American branch of the League, and intimately connected with that of Great Britain; and as somewhat a representative of both, I am remaining on the Continent, for the purpose of endeavoring to put in circulation these heavenly and precious ideas through the French and German press, and such other channels of communication with the Continental mind as I may find open for that object. Every week, I propose to send out about 200 "*Olive Leaves*" to as many continental journals, with the hope that many of the editors will read them, and a few copy them into their columns. Each *Leaf* contains a short article upon some point involved in the subject of peace.

Several journals have admitted these articles, which is encouraging. Besides this operation, I should be glad to secure the regular insertion of about 1-1/2 or *two* columns of such matter in a few leading and widely circulated journals, in different parts of Germany, every *month* by *paying* for the space occupied a reasonable *price* per line. For it is of the most importance to have a few *permanent circles of readers*, in order to make an impression. I have already arranged with several journals for a monthly insertion of these Leaves, and, in every case, they have made a reduction of from 33 to 50 per cent on their usual price per line for advertisements, some in consideration of the monthly *repetition* of the matter, others because the matter itself would be of interest to their readers. Now, thinking that you might have a widely circulated and important journal in Bremen, read extensively through the district of which it is the center, I write to ask if you would not be so good as to wait upon the editor of such a journal, and inquire on what terms he would admit one of my Leaves *regularly* every *month?* It would occupy about a column & a half of his paper, and I am quite sure it would be far more *readable* to his subscribers than ordinary *advertisement* matter. I should like to have you ascertain as nearly as you can, the number of copies issued by the journal, as that would determine the arrangement. I enclose a copy of an Olive Leaf which I should like to have him insert first, if we can make a bargain. I have marked out such articles as he might *omit*, as there is more matter than he would like to insert at once. As this matter would be *readable*, it would not crowd out any of his regular advertisements. If you will do me this favour, at your early convenience, I shall be much obliged to your kindness.

Could you, also, give me a few names of persons in Bremen, who you may think susceptible of sympathy for this movement and who, when interested, might be able to advance it? I should like to send the Bond of Brotherhood to about half a dozen persons in Bremen & vicinity who would receive and read it. And will you not read it, and acquaint yourself with the principles and plans of operation it advocates, and with the spirit of those engaged in the work? Have you no ladies who could be interested in the cause, and permit me to put them in correspondence with the ladies in England who are co-operating with enthusiastic interest, for the dissemination of these beautiful principles?

Hoping soon to hear from you

I remain yours truly

Elihu Burritt

BURRITT MSS.
Library of the Institute of New Britain

[MS. JOURNALS]

[Hamburg] Wednesday, Nov. 27 [1850]

. . . The bill for the insertion [of the Olive Leaves] in the "Nachrichten" was about 65 marks; a little less than £3. [Actually it was £2, 17 sh.] But this sum pays for the printing and distribution of at least 10,000 copies which is far cheaper than it could be done in a separate form. I feel some concern lest the first article, which is addressed particularly to the Working Classes and urging them to unite and pledge themselves not to fight, may create some suspicion in the minds of the authorities. I crossed it out in the copy, to be omitted; but it was all put in. I hope it may not attract observation or distrust.

Hotel de Bavière, Hamburgh [Nov.] 29, 1850

Rev L. S. Jacoby

My Dear Sir

I am truly obliged for your cordial and prompt answer to my letter on the subject of the "*Olive Leaves.*" It is the first object we have in view, in securing their regular insertion in several leading journals, to reach as large a circle of permanent readers as possible. It was our original intention to have them printed *seperately* in the form of the enclosed, and to have them distributed from house to house in the large cities, by persons employed for that purpose. We should prefer this plan but it seems not quite practical under the present inauspicious circumstances. Therefore, as a substitute for this plan, we now propose to secure their insertion in a few leading journals monthly. Printed *seperately* in the enclosed form, they cost about 6 English shillings per 1000. Therefore we hope to get them inserted in the journals as cheaply as if printed *separately*. For instance 5000 copies thus printed would cost 30 English shillings. Then a paper having a circulation of 5000 copies, we hope, would insert an Olive Leaf for 30 shillings; which would be at the same rate as they would cost separately. The price paid therefore, must depend upon the *circulation* of the journal. As, for instance, if we gave the "*Neue Bremen Zeitung*" 30 shillings, or 24 marks, for inserting a *Leaf*, the publisher would only give us 500 or 800 copies of it for that sum, while the Weser Zeitung, with a circulation of 4500, would give us that number of copies for the same price. We should much prefer the character of the Neue Bremen Zeitung's readers; but feel it a great object to reach as many minds as we can with our principles, and at as cheap a rate as possible. So I should be greatly obliged if you would see the editor of the *Weser Zeitung* and ask him if he will engage to insert an Olive Leaf regularly once a month, and on what terms. Each *Leaf* will make about 300 lines, occupying a column & half. The matter will consist of several short articles, some of them extracts from the speeches or writings of Statesmen and the best men of different countries & ages. It will be our effort to serve up matter which shall be read with as much interest as any selections which he would make himself. Thus, in consideration of the *character* and *amount* of the matter, I hope the editor will be disposed to admit it on conditions which we can accept. The money will always be paid by return of the post that brings us the amount. I enclose another Leaf, which you can show him. Each Leaf will contain this quantity of matter. I hope he will be disposed to arrange with us on liberal terms.

I shall be glad to send a few copies of the Bond of Brotherhood to Bremen; especially to Germans who can read English. I hope you will find in this little messenger of good-will many things which will accord with your sentiments. It is a beautiful cause and the more you put your heart in communication with its spirit, the more you will see its excellence. I hope you may feel it a privilege to enunciate these principles on all favorable opportunities and enjoy the pleasure of seeing them spread and take root & bring forth fruit around you.

Hoping to hear from you soon again

I remain Yours Sincerely

Elihu Burritt

BURRITT MSS.

Library of the Institute of New Britain

Hamburgh, Dec. 4, 1850

To the Editor of the *Illustrierte Zeitung*,

Sir:

If you could make room in your widely circulated journal for the short article herewith enclosed you would contribute thereby to disseminate useful ideas on the subject of War and its consequences. I would thank you most sincerely for inserting my article Die bebrudering der Volker. I have made mention of your generosity in publications issued in England & the United States.

I am very respectfully
Yours
Elihu Burritt

MS. COLLECTIONS
Library of The Hague Peace Palace

3 Winchester Buildings
London,
March 28, 1851

Dear Mrs. Landers

I am sure you will pardon me for writing you a few lines on a subject which, you know, is the great absorbing interest of my mind. Of all the pleasures which I experience connected with this great work of Peace & Brotherhood, none is more precious than the thought that my old friends and neighbours, of my native village, and their children, who have come to womanhood and manhood, since I resided there, so fully sympathize and unite with me in this mission. The Olive Leaf Society in New Britain is the first jewel in my earthly crown of rejoicing; it supplies me with courage, hope and faith to labour in this cause. It would increase my joy exceedingly, if members of the different churches and circles of Society in N.B. would join it; especially from the *South* Church. And I know of no one who would be welcomed with more cordiality and delight into the embrace of this sister bond than yourself. Perhaps you would be willing, at least, to attend one or two of their meetings, in order to learn more fully the spirit and object of the Society. This you could do without enrolling yourself as a member of it. Now I am going to ask one of the sisters to invite you to one of them, to spend an hour. You will not decline to go, for just *once*, will you? Remember the days of old when we all gathered into one fold, and sat down together in one house of prayer.

Sincerely yours
Elihu Burritt

BURRITT MSS.
Library of the New Britain Institute

Winchester Buildings, [London]
May 17, 1851

Miss Rebecca Harrison
My dear Friend,

I am truly glad to hear that you had such an interesting season at your little gathering on the 14th.[46] Certainly your *bill of fare* was rich and varied. I almost wonder that, with such a feast, you could be willing to defer the pleasure of feeling yourselves a *regularly organized* Society. But you will do this at your next, I am sure. I am glad you received so many nice letters. The day of your meeting passed my mind until it was too late to have all the letters sent you that I would have liked; but I hope that those received were highly acceptable to all the parties. I have just returned from a weeks tour in the Eastern Counties—have had a most satisfactory time. *Five* new societies were formed—two on Monday and two on Wednesday. Then we had besides a noble soiree at Ipswich: 150 sat down to tea. Now, my dear friend,—now that your heart is full of faith & hope in

---

[46] The gathering was that of an Olive Leaf Circle. These circles of women raised money by sewing for bazaars, and by various other means, for the insertion of the "Olive Leaves" in the Continental press.

reference to the power, beauty and progress of this heavenly cause, I want to have you strengthen your sisters, who have just come into the work. I have promised letters for all these new circles for their first meetings, which take place next week. Do please write a sisterly letter to Miss Maria Lancaster, Bury St. Edwards, one of the secretaries of the Society just formed there. If you would give her almost the same account of your interesting meeting which you sent me, it would be very encouraging and serviceable to their circle. They meet on Thursday (5th day) next, and you must write immediately, to be in season for their reunion. I will take it kind in thee if thou will do this; and I trust thou will derive much satisfaction in welcoming into our sisterhood this circle of sisters.

I hope we shall soon have a stock of the enclosed cards, but if thou art in haste for them, perhaps it will be well to write directly to James Valentine, 100 Murray Gate, Dundee, who would send thee a few by post.

Thine with
Sincere esteem,
Elihu Burritt

MS. PORTFOLIO, Vol. XXX
Friends House, London

3 Winchester Buildings, London
June 12, 1851

Charles Sumner Esq.
My dear Friend

My soul is gladdened to great & exceeding joy at the news of your election to fill the place of Daniel Webster in the U. S. Senate. I have just been reading your letter to the Mass. Legislature,[47] accepting the post, and my heart responds with an admiring *amen* to all the sentiments you express. I congratulate you on this issue of the struggle, and I feel a stronger attachment to old Massachusetts for

[47] *The Works of Charles Sumner* (Boston, 1894), Vol. II, pp. 437-440.

it. Through you our noble old state will speak in the language of its olden speech for human freedom. What a career opens before you! to speak for Massachusetts! to reproduce and re-enunciate the lofty words of her old patriots who spoke unrestricted by the subtle meshes of *Cottonocracy!* [48] Dear Sumner! be strong in the might of the right! The world expects much of you—a strong, firm, dignified speech for humanity—for Freedom, Peace, and Brotherhood. Your election has been hailed by the friends of human freedom & progress in this country with exhaltation. The *Times* has given a leader on it, which you probably have seen. There are more eyes and hearts fixed upon your course, than upon that of any man in America.

We looked forward with lively anticipation to your attending the Peace Congress in London. It would have been a noble opportunity for you to have spoken a great speech to the world. I wish it were possible for you now to attend. Our country has been barely represented on these occasions heretofore. Our delegates have been mostly those who visited Europe for pleasure; they have not prepared themselves for speaking, and have thus failed to make that impression which was expected. For all these reasons we should have your presence with gladness.

My *Citizen* is dead and buried. Its loss has been a grief to me; for it was my first born. But I hope you will look with favour upon my little magazine, "The Bond of Brotherhood," which we send you regularly. It will keep you advised of my operations on this side of the water.

Yours Ever,
Elihu Burritt

SUMNER MSS., *Letters Received*, Vol. XVI
Harvard College Library

---

[48] The term used to describe that faction of the Whig Party in Massachusetts which, because of its dependence on Southern cotton and markets, took a proslavery position on political questions.

Manchester, June 18, 1851

[To an unknown person]

Since I parted with you in London a great affliction has come down upon me and my soul is exceedingly sorrowful. Dear, good, meek, Joseph Crosfield has been suddenly called to his rest & reward. He was one of the dearest Friends I ever had on earth and my heart was never before smitten with so deep a grief as that with which I mourn his loss. I came here yesterday to attend his lifeless form to its long home, but they had laid him down in his grave before I arrived. He was to me a brother in every degree and extent of attachment. A fraternal relation & communion more intimate, more precious & sacred, than even consanguinity could inspire, united us & cemented our friendship. . . . As Jonathan loved David so clung my heart to the beauty of his character and it feels widowed at this sudden bereavement. But I would be grateful for the gift of his life so long, for the treasure and precious memory of his example that [illegible] year I have lived & labored within the atmosphere of his spirit.

Elihu Burritt

MS. FRIENDS AUTOGRAPHS, Vol. V
Friends House

3 Winchester Buildings, London, Aug. 29 1851
[To Gerrit Smith]
My Dear Friend—

The great Peace Congress and the demonstrations have so absorbed my time & thoughts for the last months that I have not been able to write you till to-day. I thank you with my whole heart for your very generous and kind donation to aid me in the great work which I have in hand. It was a gift that helped me very much, and for which I hope you may reap a rich reward. It was all the more precious to me, from the fact, that recently all my earthly possessions or property and business in America has been swept away, and a great burden rolled upon my shoulders, which must weigh heavily upon me during the rest of my life.[49] I thank you most gratefully for this new act of your goodness to me. Now that the Peace Congress is over I am giving myself to the expansion of the Olive Leaf enterprise, and the agitation of the Ocean Penny Postage question. Everything seems promising for both, and I hope the last will be realized ere long. I derive much pleasure from the thought that you receive and read regularly the Bond of Brotherhood, as it must keep you advised of our progress & proceedings

Yours Sincerely
Elihu Burritt

GERRIT MILLER SMITH COLLECTION
Syracuse University

[MS. JOURNALS]

[London] Thursday, April 8 [1852]

Rev Mr Osborne, Chaplain of the Gaol, came in to breakfast, and remained till nearly 12. He is truly an earnest man with his whole being, and life, and expression animated with great-hearted philanthropy. It was refreshing to hear him pour out his loving thoughts of goodness to the multitude of young beings pushed by poverty into crime, with no chance to recover the first step in the downward road of ruin. I developed my plan for rescuing the young vagrants in London from the sewers of sin and poverty, and setting them to cooperate with Providence in reclaiming the waste lands in the vicinity of the Metropolis, thus making their own lives productive and those acres of uncultivated wilderness now as barren as their own existence. . . .

[Lyons] Saturday, Sept. 11 [1852]

Arose to the onerous duties of my mission with a heavy heart, after a long, and almost sleepless night. . . . After breakfast, I went out and called upon Mr Hudebert, the

---

[49] The financial failure and bankruptcy of *The Christian Citizen*.

American consul, as there was none from England at Lyons. He readily entered into the object of my visit, and rendered me every assistance I could desire. Lyons is the only city in France in the same category as Paris, where the Prefect of the Department is also invested with the authority of mayor. We repaired therefore to the Hotel de la Prefecture, but found that the Prefect was in Paris. The General Secretary was then the only official who could receive the Liverpool Address. So I returned to my room and made a copy of the translation, and at 3 we waited upon him, and though he was much pressed with calls, he admitted us immediately to an audience. He was rather a young man, quick and active in his movements, and received us standing, as if he could not afford us a long interview. Mr Hudebert explained in a few words our object in calling upon him, and I entered upon my usual explanation of the object, spirit & origin of the Friendly Addresses. But before I had finished he commenced his reply, and spoke earnestly in commendation of this interchange of friendly sentiments between the two countries. He said that the Government and people of France would receive with lively sympathy these expressions of esteem and good-will on the part of the English nation; and would heartily reciprocate them. Both countries had a deep and vital interest in the maintenance of pacific relations with each other and all the world. He spoke a few minutes with much fervour in this strain, and then said that he would consult with the Prefect on his return from Paris, and they would address such a response to the communication from Liverpool as its noble sentiments deserved. I then gave him the name of Richard Rathbone to whom he might direct his letter of acknowledgment, and we took our leave, feeling gratified at the result of the interview. As we passed out we witnessed a scene illustrating the evils of war preparations. The Hotel de Ville was thronged with young men in blouse selling themselves for substitutes to fathers whose sons had been drawn to serve in the army. It resembled a slave market in some respects. Returned to my room and wrote to Edmund Fry and good Joseph Sturge. Commenced also the copies of the Liverpool address for the Lyons Journals. . . .

Monday, Sept. 13 [1852]

Arose early, and prepared the papers for the press. Called upon the American consul, who went with me to the bureau of the Courrier de Lyon, but the chief editor was not in. Left with his associate a copy of the Address, and my letter. Next proceeded to the Salut Public, where I was received with great cordiality. One of the editors seemed to [be] well acquainted with my name and operations. Took leave of Mr Hudebert, the consul, who has been very good and helpful to me, and promised to send me copies of the Lyons journals containing the Address. I then went alone to the office of the Gazette de Lyon, and had a long conversation with the editor. He thinks the people of France have taken no notice of the attacks made upon the Government by the London Times. Returned to my room, packed up for my journey, and at 1 left Lyons in a steamer for Valence.

[Nîmes] Thursday, Sept. 16 [1852]

. . . Found at the P Office 5 journals from Lyons, *Le Salut Public*, *Gazette de Lyons*, and the *Courrier*, all containing the Friendly Address from Liverpool with my letter, and editorial remarks. Those of the *Salut* were most excellent. Thus nearly the whole of the reading population of Lyons will see these noble sentiments. . . .

[Paris] Wednesday, Oct. 6 [1852]

This was a sad day for me. My headache was so completely prostrating, that I was obliged to keep my bed until night. But I could review my long journey, and all its incidents, anxieties and labours with a feeling of satisfaction and gratitude. I feel that this mission has been one of the most important and interesting that I ever undertook. The tokens of Divine favour which have attended it have been marked and numerous. It will always constitute a chapter in my experience to which I shall revert with pleasure. . . .

[London] Saturday, July 9 [1853]

Wrote a few letters, then went with Henry Richard on a mission I had proposed, or to the American minister to ask him to interpose a proposition of arbitration between the Great Powers that seem to be on the eve of open hostilities on the Turkey Question. The United States is the only first rate nation in Christendom that is not involved in this question, therefore the best situated for offering to mediate. We unfortunately did not find Mr. Ingersoll[50] at home, and were told he was to leave town for the country in the afternoon. We then proceeded to James Bells, and wrote the following letter which we left at the Ministers requesting its earliest delivery:

To his Excellency, J. R. Ingersoll

In the present critical conjuncture of affairs in the East of Europe, the Friends of Peace in this country are extremely solicitous that some means should be found to divert so terrible a disaster as a war among the great powers could not fail to prove to the interests of civilization throughout the world. It has appeared to some of them that no expedient would so much conduce to this end, as the friendly interposition of some state of equal political standing with those that are at variance, but whose independence and neutrality would enable it to adjudicate, without any suspicion of partiality or interested motives. In the present case, none of the *great* nations of Europe are in this neutral position. But it seems to us that the United States are invested with all the qualities which would confer authority upon and inspire confidence in such a mediation as we have

[50] Joseph Reid Ingersoll (1786-1868), son of Jared Ingersoll, Whig member of Congress, Minister to Great Britain from 1852 to 1853.

indicated. The unanimous report recently presented to the American Senate by the Committee on Foreign Relations, strongly recommending the general principle of arbitration as a means of solving international disputes, gives us ground to hope that an offer of friendly services on your part, at this momentous emergency, could not fail to secure the cordial approbation of the Government you represent.

We trust you will pardon our importunity, if we venture urgently to request the honour of an interview at your earliest convenience, with the view to state at greater length than is possible in this note, the sentiment of those on whose behalf we are acting on the present occasion. We shall hold ourselves in readiness to wait upon your Excellency at any time and place you may please to appoint.

We have the honour to be Your Excellency's humble & Obedient Servants,

Henry Richard
Elihu Burritt

Tuesday, July 12. [1853]

At 4 P. M. Mr. Richard & myself were at the American Minister's, and found him at home. He received us very cordially, without any diplomatic stiffness or formality, and seemed a plain, common sense man, full of practical sentiments. I introduced Mr Richard, and the subject of our interview, and dwelt at length upon the propriety and necessity of an offer of mediation on the part of the United States through him. I urged the fact that all the great powers of Europe of a status to mediate had been drawn into the Eastern Controversy; that the United States were the only neutral power, and they could most gracefully interpose a proposition of arbitration. Referred also to the recent action in the U. S. Senate in favour of Arbitration,[51]

[51] On February 5, 1851, Senator Henry Foote reported a resolution from the Committee on Foreign Relations indicating the desirability of governmental action in securing arbitration clauses in treaties with foreign powers.

as giving him authority to step forward and propose this
mode of settlement. Mr Richard urged these and other considerations upon him. He then expressed his mind very
fully upon the point; saying that such an interposition on
the part of the U. S. had never occurred to him until he received our note. He heartily commended our object, and appreciated the gravity of the question. Still he doubted
whether he could act except *conditionally* in the matter,
until he could receive instructions from the U. S. Government. He thought he might do this. Another interview
was appointed for Thursday and we left, after a conversation of 1-½ hour.

Thursday, July 14 [1853]

. . . At 4 I went to the American Ministers, where I
joined Mr Cobden and Richard. We had a long conversation with Mr Ingersoll on the subject of his offering the
mediation of the U. S. in the Eastern Question. He seemed
quite disposed to do so, but rather shrank from the responsibility of making an advance without the previous sanction of our Govt. After a long and earnest discussion of
the propriety and necessity of the step, he expressed his
willingness to speak to Baron Brunow, and offer the mediation of the U. S. Government conditional on its acceptance
of the service. . . .[52]

[52] Ingersoll felt unable to offer the services of his government for reasons
indicated in the following letter to Burritt.
  J. R. Ingersoll to Elihu Burritt   45 Portland Place
                     July 25, 1853
. . . Nothing could be gained if it should be followed by that support, and
much would be lost if that support should be withheld.
 The difficulty at present is, that in doing all you desire, I should be creating instructions, which is almost the same thing as defeating them. Rest
assured that there is no harm in the present posture, as you will be fully
satisfied when it is known to you. In the meantime you will be good enough to
understand that what you have said and written has not been thrown away
upon
         Your faithful and most Obedient Servant,
             J. R. Ingersoll

[Leipsig] Saturday Sept. 10 [1853]

. . . I next went to the office of the *Illustrierte Zeitung* which has published our Olive Leaves from the beginning. The editor received me cordially, and on my asking him to write an article in favour of Ocean Penny Postage, he showed me one of two columns length in proof, which he had written for that very number. . . . Mr. Weber came in, the proprietor of the journal, and a large publisher of illustrated literature, and gave me a hearty welcome. We had a long conversation upon the proposition which I submitted, to bring out an illustrated monthly paper for Workingmen and their Families, the same size as the Band of Hope, and nearly of the same character. I offered to edit it, to furnish all the matter and even to have it all translated ready for the press, without any charge, if he would publish it on his own pecuniary responsibility. I urged that we could serve up a spicy variety of matter, which would make the publication a welcome visitor to thousands of German workingmen, women and children and to the homes of the people generally. He thought it would be impossible to bring it out for "half penny" like the Band of Hope, but I suggested that it might pay well at one *grosschen*. He said he would give the subject his serious consideration, and I engaged to send him a copy of the Band of Hope on my return to England. He seemed quite favourably disposed towards the enterprise, and said he shared fully with us a regard for the principles of Peace. He had sometimes thought of publishing our Olive Leaves in the form of a book, but feared the Government might trouble him if he did it.

[London] Friday, Oct. 7 [1853]

Received a letter today from Mr Weber, accepting my proposition to bring out a monthly magazine in German. He seems to enter upon this enterprise with much good feeling and confidence. This is almost embarrassing, though encouraging. For I must leave most of the arrangement until I reach America. I intend to send a few articles to Henrietta Braus for translation. . . .

[New Britain] Wed. Nov. 2 [1853]
Wrote again for the new German periodical, and made a little progress. This is a weighty and arduous undertaking, considering my other engagements, but I hope I may be able to accomplish it without great trouble. It is a novel task truly, to edit a magazine in a foreign tongue and country, but I trust it may be useful. The relation it will establish between me and a large circle of families in Germany will be intimate and responsible. . . .

Monday Nov. 7. [1853]
. . . . Find that the Bond and the new German magazine, which I have called the *Wohlvollensbote* will occupy at least half of my time. But I believe it is the best disposition I can make of my strength. . . .

Monday. Dec. 19. [1853]
Wrote all day for the *Wohlvollensbote*, as I must send all the articles for the February no by the next steamer. . . .

[Washington] Friday, March 24 [1854]
Arose with one of my old headaches upon me, owing to writing too long yesterday, and perhaps the excitement of the "*spiritual* manifestations" [by Linton, the Quaker medium] last evening. This was very unfortunate as I was to dine at the Presidents. Kept my bed most of the time till 4, when I went to the "White House". After waiting in the receiving room with two gentlemen for a few minutes, the President came in, and was very affable and cordial.[53] After introducing me to the two other guests, he sat down by me, and commenced a lively conversation; first enquiring if I still pursued the study of languages & then entering

[53] The standard biography of Franklin Pierce is that of Roy Nichols, *Franklin D. Pierce* (Philadelphia, 1931).

upon the subject of peace. I was almost surprised at the
force and emphasis of his declarations in reference to this
question. He said no one could more fully appreciate the
miseries of war than he who had witnessed them with his
own eyes and taken part in its scenes. He felt for himself
an intense abhorrence of the system not only for its horrors,
but for its folly. It could not settle any question of controversy. The contending powers must come to negotiation
or arbitration at last, after all their fighting. Why should
they not then resort to this method of adjudication before
resorting to arms. He said that at the present stage of
civilization, one power did not expect to extinguish or make
a conquest of the other, but that their sovereignty and integrity should be retained, whatever might be the issue
of the struggle. This circumstance made arbitration all
the more reasonable and necessary. He continued in this
strain for a few minutes, when I remarked, that his views
must coincide with those presented in our Peace Congresses
in behalf of Arbitration and other substitutes for war; and
asked if he could not approve of stipulated Arbitration, as
advocated on those occasions. He said the difficulty would be
in finding impartial arbitrators, especially in a case in
which the United States were concerned, intimating that
the European powers would directly or indirectly commit
themselves in favor of the European party in the controversy. He referred to their interference with the people
and interest of the American Continent, as a case which arbitration would not reach, and in which war, with all its horrors, would be a less calamity than yielding to this interference. He said that these powers must "keep their hands
off" from this continent, and that so long as he remained
in his present position, he should deem it his imperative
duty to enforce the "Monroe doctrine." I asked if it was
his opinion that this doctrine should be enforced retrospec-
tively. He replied with much emphasis certainly not. The

present possessions of European powers in North America, and its waters, should be respected, but that no new ones should be acquired, and no arrangements organized to impede the expansion of the United States in any legitimate direction. He alluded with a good deal of earnestness to the intimation of alliance between England & France to prevent the acquisition of Cuba by the United States, lying as it did in the immediate pathway of our commerce and connection with the Pacific states of the Union. He seemed to regard the attempt of these powers to maintain the possession of that island for Spain as an effort to blockade and bar the highway of our intercourse in the Gulf of Mexico.

When I suggested that those powers might conceive their own West India possessions imperilled by the annexation of Cuba to the United States, he said that there could be no just grounds of such apprehension on their part. In connection with this and the Fishery Question, he referred to the proneness of the people of all countries for war and warlike manifestation. He intimated that Mr Crampton [the British Minister] had felt this to be a difficulty.

Here Mrs Pierce and Mrs Means entered the room, and the conversation on these points was suspended. . . . . [At dinner] they all asked many questions in reference to my sojourn and experience in Europe. This gave me a good opportunity to describe the Ocean Penny Postage Movement in England, and to mention many incidents illustrating the bearing of the present high rates upon the poor. I referred to the "show of hands" that was taken at the conclusion of the public meetings to ascertain how many had friends beyond the sea. The President listened to these particulars with lively manifestations; occasionally mentioning a fact in evidence of the importance and value of cheap ocean postage. Conversation turned upon the visit of the English Friends, and the President spoke of them in terms of great respect. Mrs Pierce said they had presented her quite a library of biographies of distinguished members of their Society, which she anticipated much gratification in reading. I then adverted to the mission of Joseph Sturge and his companions to St Petersburgh;[54] to their interview with the Emperor and Empress, and to the cause and extent of the influence which English Friends had with that court; referring especially to Daniel Wheeler and Wm Allen.

I also spoke of the character and labor of the late Wm Forster, of his philanthropic and self-sacrificing labours in Ireland, during the famine in that country; of his mission to various courts of Europe, and to other illustrations of his devotion to the glory of God and the good of men. After dinner, returning to the receiving room, the President retired to his official business, shaking all the guests cordially by the hand. We remained a few minutes in conversation with the ladies, and I explained briefly the Olive Leaf Movement, and the interest and activity which the ladies in Great Britain had manifested in the dessemination of the ideas of peace at home and abroad. I gave them copies of our little publications upon the subject, and then took my leave, much gratified at the interest.

Monday, April 2 [1854]

Wrote a letter to the President, urging him to offer his mediation to the contending powers of Europe. . . .

Sir.—With sincere and profound respect, I venture to solicit your favorable consideration of a subject of the most intense importance to the well-being of the whole human race. In as few words as possible I will endeavor to present it.

A few weeks before leaving England, I made one of a deputation, including Richard Cobden, who waited upon Hon J. R. Ingersoll, our Minister in London, for the pur-

---

[54] This was an effort on the part of British Friends to prevent the Crimean War.

pose of requesting him to offer the mediation of the United States between Russia and Turkey. We had two long interviews with that gentleman, and urged all the arguments which we could derive from the circumstances of this momentous and perilous controversy, to induce him to take this step towards its peaceful adjustment. He gave to the proposition the most serious and sympathetic consideration.

He acknowledged the force and pertinence of all our arguments, and fully admitted that the United States were the only nation on the earth whose mediation would be likely to be satisfactory and successful. He gave us to understand that personally he should esteem it an honor to be the medium of communicating such an offer to the contending powers; but that he could not do it without the special authority and direction of the Government of the United States. Immediately after our last interview, I addressed him a long letter, urging considerations more *American* in their significance and application than I was willing to present in the hearing of Mr Cobden and the rest of the deputation. He admitted the full force of these, but still, with renewed and more emphatic expressions of regret, he felt constrained to decline our request, for the lack of that authority which would alone make the offer of American mediation of any value.

And now I would venture to solicit the attention of your Excellency to the proposition we submitted to Mr Ingersoll. All the considerations urged upon him in favor of American mediation, have since that time acquired new force. All the Powers of Europe, that have any political influence, have been drawn into this impending struggle, by some direct interest in its issue at least. Hence they are totally disqualified for the service of impartial mediation or arbitration. The United States, then, are the only Power in Christendom whose *status* and position would inspire confidence in the justice and impartiality of its arbitrament.

In the last great European Conflict, commencing with the events of 1793, our young Republic still ranked, in population and influence, among the minor nations of the world. But now it has attained its august majority; and with what act or manifestation of more moral grandeur could it inaugurate that majority, than by stepping in, at this momentous crisis, between the great Powers of Europe, and with a beneficent hand of impartial good-will and equity, staying a conflict which threatens to involve the progress and civilization of the age in a bloody abyss of ruin! None of your illustrious predecessors in the Presidential chair ever filled it at such an important conjunction of human affairs as that which now, under Providence, may be guided and determined by your single hand. It can hardly be possible that any of your successors will ever see such a conjuncture. With almost a feeling of awe at the vast and magnificent importance that attaches to your position at this great crisis of the world's history, I would beg your Excellency to distinguish your administration by an act which would cover our common country with a glory it has never won or worn, and which would associate your name with an estimation more precious than all the laurels won in war up to the present day.

In as few words as possible, I have ventured to present this important subject for your consideration. May He who turneth the nations as the rivers of water are turned, incline you to offer your mediation at this solemn juncture. The friends of peace in England have done their utmost to bring about a pacific adjustment. Their efforts have failed; and their last hope, under the interposition of Providence, hangs upon your personal action. If you should be willing to communicate through your minister in London or Paris an offer of mediation a contest involving immeasurable catastrophes may perhaps be avoided.

E[lihu] B[urritt]

35 Broad Street Buildings, London
Oct. 18, 1854

My dear Miss Rowntree,

I have recently returned from America, and am now writing to the circles in England, to enquire how they progress. I earnestly hope that the Olive Leaf Circle in Scarboro is still in an active state of organization; that you still keep up your meetings with spirit; that you find them seasons of profitable enjoyment, and of great utility to the cause. We earnestly hope that none of your members have suffered themselves to be discouraged by this lamentable war [the Crimean War] but that you have derived new & powerful motives for increased activity in disseminating our principles among the people of all nations. If you see the Bond of Brotherhood regularly, you will have observed in the October no. a proposition to *double* our operations on the Continent; am sure this plan will commend itself to your sympathy. Several of the circles have readily & generously responded to this project, & we are already making the requisite arrangements. I enclose a couple of the circulars we prepared for distribution in collecting for this special enterprize. Hoping soon to receive a few lines at least from your circle

I am truly Yours,
Elihu Burritt

MS. PORTFOLIO, Vol. XVIII
Friends House Library

[MS. JOURNALS]

Thursday, Jan. 4, [1855]

. . . . Have written an article, . . . on the proposition to annex the Sandwich Islands.[55] I have dwelt upon the consequences of this step, as inaugurating a colonial policy

[55] See M. E. Curti, "Young America," *American Historical Review*, Vol. XXXII (Oct., 1926), pp. 34-55.

kindred to that of Great Britain. I have admitted the probability of the whole Continent of North America becoming absorbed into the Union; but have tried to describe some of the results of acquiring territories beyond the Continent. But if this should be accomplished, I have urged the duty of paying a full, honest and satisfactory price for every acre.

Wednesday, Jan. 10 [1855]

Continued writing on my article, entitled "The Duty and Dignity of the United States as a Nationality" in which I dwelt upon the importance of forming an independent opinion of European affairs, and of maintaining a neutral attitude and an impartial mind towards the countries involved in this contest [the Crimean War]. I feel persuaded that the American mind has been nullified in its influence by being impregnated with British prejudices; by adopting the views of the London journals. This article may be unpleasant to some of my English friends, but I hope they will see that it is written in the best spirit.

CHAPTER III

THE CAMPAIGN FOR OCEAN PENNY POSTAGE

WHEN Burritt arrived in England in 1846 there was a fairly widespread feeling in philanthropic circles, as well as among certain business groups, that the rates of domestic postage ought to be considerably reduced. It occurred to the American reformer that a great boon would be conferred upon the poor immigrants in America and their friends in Europe if the charges for carrying letters across the ocean itself were reduced—the cost of sending a letter between America and Europe was twenty-five cents.[1] In addition, cheaper international postage would promote the cause of universal peace by facilitating communication and by diminishing prejudice and misunderstanding. Burritt wrote his first pamphlet on ocean penny postage in 1846, and this project became one of the major enterprises of the League of Universal Brotherhood. For ten years, Burritt wrote later, he "rode that idea up and down the United Kingdom and the United States with all the persistent hope and faith of any enthusiastic hobby-rider."[2]

In view of the details in the following letters and selections from the *Journal*, it is hardly necessary even to outline the scope and intensity of Burritt's labors in behalf of this cause. He addressed 150 huge meetings in

---

[1] *Bond of Brotherhood*, new series, no. 45, April, 1854, p. 137.
[2] Elihu Burritt, *Ten Minute Talks on All Sorts of Topics* (London, 1874), p 660.

Great Britain, and from these meetings petitions were sent to Parliament in behalf of British initiative in effecting an international agreement for cheap ocean postage. John Bright, who on one occasion spoke from the same platform for the same cause, declared that his "facts were convincing and his language beautiful and impressive." [3] Burritt lived to see his essential aim realized, and there can be little doubt that his labors contributed substantially to the victory.

[3] *The Diaries of John Bright, with a foreword by Philip Bright* (London, 1930), pp. 132-133.

35 Broad Street Buildings
London, Nov. 7, 1851

My dear Charles Sumner,

It almost seems to me as if the great boon of an *Ocean Penny Postage* were in arm's length of its realisation, when you "embrace the measure with your whole heart." I believe with the agitation we are now organizing in this country, and *Te duce* in the U. S. Senate, we shall be able to carry it through the next session of Parliament and of Congress. Every thing is working well toward it. The public mind here is most favorably disposed toward it; public men are ready to act for it; there is no opposition, economical, political, or religious. *Protectionists,* Free Traders, Tories and Radicals, Churches, Dissenters, Protestants and Catholics, are ready to lend it a helping hand. We have two excellent agencies for moving the Government and people here. In the first place we have the League of Brotherhood, with its 100 active auxiliary societies disseminated and busy in all the considerable towns of the Kingdom, "manufacturing public opinion" in favor of the measure. I and our secretary, Edmund Fry, intend to give ourselves to the addressing public meetings on the subject, getting up petitions to Parliament etc. Already several Chambers of Commerce have memorialized, or are about to memorialize, Parliament in favor of the boon. Hon. Milner Gibson,[4] once a member of the Cabinet, will, we expect, bring forward a motion in the House early in the session, and we trust to sustain him with 1000 petitions from different towns and communities. So much for our operations, connected with the League of Brotherhood. Then a great international committee has been formed, consisting of several members of Parliament, and representatives of Foreign Governments, Lord Ashburton [5] is at the head of this I believe. They will

[4] Thomas Milner Gibson (1806-1884), liberal British statesman and advocate of free trade.

[5] William Bingham Baring, second Baron Ashburton (1799-1864).

operate directly upon Governments to induce them to *concur* with a proposition for such a reduction. Now then if you will take it up in the Senate of the United States I am sure it might be passed through without much delay, for it must be a measure coming within the province of the treaty-making power. You will have a great organized force of public opinion with you. It is a measure vast and grand and good, like the great Exhibition perpetuated into a universal condition. Barnabas Bates,[6] the Rowland Hill of America, writes enthusiastically on the subject. He says he will throw himself into the measure with all his heart, and he thinks all the Cheap Postage Associations will do the same. He is going to reproduce our illustrated envelopes in his own work, "if they cannot be brought out otherwise." I write to him by this post, expressing the hope that he will marshall his activities and organisations under you, and sustain you with the force of public opinion necessary for carrying the measure. You will need an out-of-doors agitator and general. Last session I sent several of the Ocean Penny Pamphlets to members of both Houses, and wrote to 20 of them by one post. I have very cordial answers from Gov. Seward, Chase & others, promising their cooperation. I will see Milner Gibson, and shall hope to have something to communicate next post from him. It would be well if a little concert of action should be instituted between you. If we can carry the measure between America and Great Britain, it is sure for the world. I send you one of my pamphlets. The small tract *"Will it Pay?"* we are distributing by the thousands. I will enclose a few of our envelopes as specimens of the instrumentalities we employ in holding up the idea to the public.[7] More than a *million* of them have been put in circulation.

 ⁶ Barnabas Bates (1785-1853), clergyman, journalist and pioneer in postal reform in the United States.
 ⁷ The envelope bore illustrations of an ocean sailing vessel and of clasped hands.

Now, dear Sumner, the wistful eye of humanity is looking to you; its great beating heart pulsates with a great hope of your championship in the Senate. God bless you, says and prays my heart with fervent aspiration. You have come to this great position in a sublime crisis. God grant you strength and wisdom to stand strong in the breach for freedom, truth & humanity.

Yours most heartily
Elihu Burritt

SUMNER MSS., *Letters Received*, Vol. XVII
Harvard College Library

35 Broad Street Buildings
London, Jan. 2 1852

Hon. Charles Sumner.

My Dear Friend

I have just returned from a most successful campaign in Lancashire in connection with the Ocean Penny Postage movement. Everywhere the subject has been received with deep sympathy. Men of all political parties and religious denominations have come forward and given the project their hearty support. Next week I am to commence a new campaign in Yorkshire. A most important meeting of the leading men and merchants of Manchester is to be called by the Mayor on the 6th, to hear an exposition of the project from me, and to give the movement a status and impetus which shall make it vigorous and successful. We expect that £500 will be subscribed in Manchester to support the agitation. Tomorrow I am to see Rt. Hon. T. Milner Gibson in reference to his bringing forward a motion in Parliament. We shall try to arrange to have this motion brought forward about the last of April, that we may have full 3 months in which to stir up the people. Up to that time I expect to address 5 public meetings a week on the subject. We hope to get 1000 petitions presented to Parliament, and many from the Colonies.

So you see we have commenced in earnest, and I shall
hope to keep you advised of our plans and progress. In all
the public meetings I have addressed I have said that you
were going to take up the measure in the American Senate,
and advocate it with all your commanding eloquence and
energy. This statement has always "drawn down the house"
in applause. I shall show your letter to Milner Gibson to-
morrow; and I have heard that he has been highly gratified
to learn that you were going to take up the subject in the
American Senate. The Continental Governments, just at
this time, will not be disposed to create any new facilities
of intercourse between their subjects and the British &
Americans.

But if we can establish Ocean Penny Postage between
Great Britain and North America, it will soon follow
in all other directions. Suppose we should concentrate
upon this department for awhile? We can bring the British
and American Governments into ready cooperation in establishing Ocean Penny Postage across the Atlantic; and
if we can realise it for this great distance it is secure for
the whole world. Perhaps you will deem it preferable to
make a distinct motion in the Senate for the American
Government to concur and cooperate with the British in
establishing an Ocean Penny Postage between the two countries. I would be greatly obliged for a few lines from you
at your early convenience on this subject, as I should be
glad if all our operations here could harmonise completely
with yours.

I hope Mr Barnabas Bates will enter upon the out-of-
door work, of interesting the public mind in the question;
thus rendering you all the aid in his power. I write to him
by this mail to this effect. I hope he will communicate with
you on the subject. As soon as I can get a list of the members of both Houses of Congress, I intend to send each a
copy of my pamphlet on Ocean Penny Postage.

You have now the illustrious Kossuth with you. I can

easily fancy the effect of his giant, glowing thoughts, put forth in overpowering eloquence. But I hope no other power than that of truth & right will be arrayed even against the despotisms of the Continent. They can face armies better and more safely than the great public opinion of the world, expressed as it has been here.

Ever & Truly Yours
Elihu Burritt

SUMNER MSS., *Letters Received*, Vol. XVIII
Harvard College Library

35 Broad Street Buildings
London, July 2, 1852

My Dear Friend Sumner,

Will you please glance at the short article in the *Bond of Bro.[therhood]* on Ocean Penny Postage? It will show you that the question has been fairly launched as a proposition in Parliament. It has not been brought forward in a formal motion, as I anticipated; but perhaps it is all for the best. Now we shall go to work for the next session; and before Parliament meets again, we shall have a gulf stream of public opinion ready to pour upon it in favour of the measure. Now the world looks to *you* for the leadership in the U. S. Congress in this reform. We will carry it *next* session of the two parliaments. Now let me entreat you to nail the flag of *1 penny* ocean postage to your masthead, and never strike or lower it. There is power in the very word *penny*. I know not how long Congress is to sit; but I earnestly hope that you will prepare yourself for bringing forward a regular motion next session of Congress. It will be a glorious thing for you to associate with your first senatorial efforts. I know you can see the blessings it will bring to millions, who will bless you for it. I send herewith an article to the New York Journal of Commerce [8] on the sub-

---

[8] The New York *Journal of Commerce*, founded by Arthur Tappan, was at this time edited by Gerard Hallock, former editor of the Boston *Telegraph*.

ject, which I hope you will see; as it contains the report of John Bright's remarks in the House, on introducing the subject. I intend to keep the question alive in the N. Y. papers.

General Election comes on next week here and we shall have stirring times.

Yours Ever & Truly

Elihu Burritt

SUMNER MSS., *Letters Received*, Vol. XIX
Harvard College Library

Nov 2, 1852

35 Broad Street Buildings [London]

My dear Sumner,

My heart yearns to bless you for that magnificent speech in the Senate on the Fugitive Slave Bill.[9] I could and did weep for joy and admiration while reading it. I am glad and proud that you spoke such words in the ear of the world. How I should have leaped for exultation if I could have listened to you. I wish you would send me a copy with your own hand.

Now will you not buckle on your armour again as the champion of Ocean Penny Postage in the Senate! We are opening the campaign here in right good counsel. I hope you will see the N Y *Journal of Commerce* to which I have just written on the subject. Let me entreat you to nail *One Penny* to the mast head. We have done it on this side of the ocean; and let us sail and fight under one flag. I will try to write you again next week.

Ever yours,

Elihu Burritt

SUMNER MSS., *Letters Received*, Vol. XX
Harvard College Library

[9] *Appendix to the Congressional Globe for the 1st Session, 32nd Congress* (Vol. XXV), pp. 1102-1113 (Washington, 1852).

35 Broad Street Buildings, London, March 11, 1853

My Dear Sumner,

I hope you keep your eye upon what we are doing for Ocean Penny Postage on this side of the water, and that you have lost not an iota of interest in this great reform. I suppose the session of Congress is now at an end, and that you are now in Boston again. But you know that we look to you as the champion of Ocean Penny Postage in the Senate. If I live and my health is continued, I intend to return to America early in next autumn, and take the field in favour of this measure. The British Government has just made a move in the right direction between it and all its colonies. It has proposed to them a uniform rate of 6ᵈ, for a letter from any town in the Colonies to any town in the United Kingdom; to be divided in this way—1ᵈ for the *inland* service in the mother country, 1ᵈ for the colonial inland, and 4ᵈ for the ocean transit. This is going just *half* way to Ocean Penny Postage between Great Britain and its colonies. I have just sent an article to the New York Journal of Commerce on the subject, and will you please glance at it, as you will probably find it [in] the reading room you visit, about a couple of days after you receive this note. If you will read it, then I need not repeat here, what it would be otherwise necessary to state. I want earnestly to entreat you to go for nothing short of Ocean *Penny* Postage. Let us nail that to the mast. It will be a glorious reform when carried, and it will associate you with the most grateful recollections in the minds of millions in America. I think we can make a successful agitation in favour of the scheme next season. I hope to speak to many public meetings on the subject in different parts of the Union. Barnabas Bates will co-operate, and other earnest and influential men. But *you* must be our leader in Congress. You stand committed to this by your own sympathy, and we must rely upon you. If we can establish an Ocean Penny Postage between Great Britain and the United States, it must follow in every other direction. I am sure the British Government will go as far as ours in the matter. So let us make a great movement next season, and the boon will be secured.

I have now presented the subject in almost every large town in the Kingdom; have spoken to 125 public meetings during the last 18 months. Everywhere it has been received with intense sympathy.

Ere many months roll around, I hope to see you again face to face. How swiftly these years roll by! It seems but yesterday since I said *goodbye* the last time. Your noble speech on the Fugitive Slave Bill is being reprinted in this country, and I hope will have a large circulation. I should be very happy to receive a few lines from you, whenever you can spare a leisure moment.

Yours ever & faithfully
Elihu Burritt

SUMNER MSS., *Letters Received*, Vol. XXI
Harvard College Library

[MS. JOURNALS]

[London] Saturday, April 16 [1853]

This was, as it were, an observation day in my experience; a day in which I seemed to have reached an advance point, from which the past and the future could be contemplated with much satisfaction. Returned to town, and at 12 was at the rooms of the Society of Arts, where the Deputation to Lord Aberdeen [10] was to meet. . . Several were present from a great distance, among whom were Henry Ashworth [11] of Bolton, and Howard Malcolmson of Manchester. Many members of Parliament came in, Milner Gibson, among others. While we waited for all to arrive,

[10] George Hamilton Gordon, fourth Earl of Aberdeen (1784–1860), was Prime Minister 1852–1858.

[11] Henry Ashworth (1794–1880), friend of Cobden and supporter of the Anti-Corn Law League.

I had a good deal of conversation with several distinguished persons. A little before 1 we took up our line of march for Downing Street and were soon densely crowded in the ante-room of the Prime Minister of the British Empire. . . Thomas Hankey, late Governor of the Bank of England was deputed to introduce the subject of the interview, and then we all proceeded up stairs to the salon of the Premier; and we were quite a regiment indeed. I was among the last, but got a good place for seeing and hearing. . . . . There were more than 80 M. P.s present, and a large number of influential merchants of London, and representatives of different Chambers of Commerce in different parts of the country.

Thomas Hankey addressed Lord Aberdeen at consider-able length, stating the object of the Deputation; and urging many forcible arguments in favour of the establish-ment of a uniform 3d rate between the mother country and the colonies . . . . Milner Gibson then addressed the Premier and stated that two associations had been formed and had laboured for the reduction of postage between Great Britain and all other countries. One of these had ad-vocated the establishment of a mere penny rate for the ocean transit, leaving the inland charges of different countries untouched. The other, or the Colonial Postage Association, had advocated the extension of the inland penny postage of the mother country to the colonies. . . . . This was a scene of the deepest interest to me. I could hardly realise that this great company of influential men had waited upon the Premier merely to urge the very proposition which I had launched upon the tide of public opinion in 1846. It was indeed very encouraging, and I desire to feel grateful to God that I am permitted to see this project approxi-mating to its full consummation. The Cheap Colonial Post-age Association and the League of Brotherhood are now one and the same in reference to this postal reform in prin-ciple, and I hope we may unite in action.

Friday, April 22 [1853]

. . . . At 7 went with Joseph Sturge to the House of Commons, where we had a long and full conversation with Cobden and Bright on the subject of Ocean Penny Postage. Both were very cordial, and quite ready to encourage Gibson to go forward and bring on his motion during the present session. Bright thinks he had better move for a Committee of Inquiry, which would be easily obtained. . .

Friday, May 20 [1853]

. . . At the close of the meeting [at Devonshire House] I came away without stopping to speak with friends, as I had engaged to meet Mr Gibson at 1-½ at the House of Commons. I found him pretty earnest in the question; and we went into a small room in the House, and prepared an answer to Mr Gladstone's letter and the Statement of Lord Canning. I wrote the words as Mr. Gibson dictated them. While I was doing this, I could not refrain from dwelling upon that mysterious leading of Providence which had brought me from the humblest obscurity of physical labour in the humblest village in America, to be closeted in this way with a distinguished member of the British Parliament in the capital of the Imperial Parliament, preparing with him a great measure which should deeply affect the social and political relations between Great Britain and all the nations of the earth. The letter to Mr Gladstone was to remove the objections to a Committee of Inquiry. If this is not conceded before next Tuesday, Mr Gibson will move for its appointment in the House. . . . .

35 Broad Street Buildings, London, July 15,
1853

Dear Friend Sumner,

I had intended ere this to acknowledge the receipt of your most interesting and welcome letters, but have been waiting to have something more definite to communicate in reference to our operations here. First in regard to

Ocean Penny Postage—Mr Gibson balloted for a night on which to bring the question before the House of Commons, but so many other questions obtained the precedency for that evening that he was obliged to postpone it. But he has declared in the House that he will bring it forward in some shape this session. In the meanwhile we are agitating in favour of the measure in different ways. We have adopted a new expedient—that is, putting up a large placard, containing the principal arguments in favour of the project in all the large towns in the Kingdom. We have arranged to put them up in 50 of the principal railway stations. This will put forth the idea very strikingly and make a deep impression on the public mind. I send you a copy of this placard, which perhaps you will see mounted on a board and put conspicuously in some central place. I sent one to Barnabas Bates last week and to Amasa Walker, and hope they will put them up in Boston. The Government here is yielding to the pressure for cheap ocean postage and I am quite confident we shall carry it next session of Parliament. We are operating here through the press very effectually. Also, once a fortnight we send about a dozen short articles to papers in America. Now in a few weeks I expect to set my face towards America again and look forward to your taking up this question in earnest in the Senate next session. I hope I and Bates may stir up a strong interest in favour of it out of doors. Do you see some of my little pieces in the American journals on the subject?

I showed your last letter to Mr Cobden, and he was well pleased at your commendation of his pamphlet, and wished me to convey to you his acknowledgment and to say how cheering it was to him to receive your sympathy and approbation. . . .

> Yours Ever
> Elihu Burritt

SUMNER MSS., *Letters Received*, Vol. XXII
Harvard College Library

[MS. JOURNALS]

Friday, Aug. 6 [1853]

. . . Last night Milner Gibson again introduced the subject of O. P. P., and asked the Chancellor if he thought there would be any objection to the appointment of a Committee to inquire into the general question of colonial and foreign postage in the early part of next session. The Chancellor, after adverting to the Gov't proposal to the colonies, which was being accepted, said "It seemed inadvisable at present to give a pledge on the subject but the subject of ocean postage was a fit one for Parliamentary inquiry, and he should be glad to see that enquiry instituted next session." . . .

New Britain, Conn.
Nov. 15, 1853

Dear Sumner

I am again *at home*, in the village of my nativity, glad again to be on American ground. I arrived here on the 29th of October, and have been much absorbed in meeting, and visiting with my relatives and friends. I am now preparing myself to take the field for the Ocean Penny Postage campaign immediately after Thanksgiving. I hope to address public meetings on the subject in all the large towns, also to get a hearing at the State Legislatures. Would not memorials from these bodies be very influential? I hope we may pour a stream of continuous petitions upon Congress from the beginning of the session. Now will you not begin to buckle on your armour as the champion of this great postal reform? I intend to go to Washington to *lobby* a little with the M. C.'s in favor of this measure. Perhaps I may not see you until I meet you there. Will you kindly drop me a few lines just to say when you will be passing through here toward Washington? Have you read the noble speeches of Cobden and Bright at the Peace Congress in Edinburgh? If not, I will send you a paper containing them.

Yours ever,

Elihu Burritt

SUMNER MSS., *Letters Received*, Vol. XXII
Harvard College Library

New Britain, Conn., Nov. 18, 1853

[Probably to Gerrit Smith]
My Dear Sir,

I am again *at home*, in my own native village, after an absence of three years in Europe. I hope to take the field in behalf of Ocean Penny Postage about the 1st of December, and address public meetings on the subject, and *agitate* by pen and speech, through the press and on the platform. I intend also to go to Washington next month for the purpose of trying to make a little interest among the M. C.'s in favour of the scheme. I am sure you will sympathize and cooperate in this work. I am very poor, but hope to work my own way from town to town and state to state by lecturing on the subject. I should like to send one of my little tracts to 300 or 400 journals, asking the editor to read and notice the proposition. I brought a good number with me from England.

I wish you would go into limited or silent partnership with me in this little undertaking. I will find paper and envelopes, and write 100 notes to as many editors, if you will *pay the postage*. I think $3 spent in this way would be a good investment.

I hope you will pardon me for this suggestion; my spirit and flesh are willing, but "silver & gold have I none."

Yours ever truly,

Elihu Burritt

MS. MISCELLANEOUS COLLECTIONS
Massachusetts Historical Society

North Brookfield, Mass.
Dec. 7, 1853

Dear Mr Sumner

I have just opened the campaign for Ocean Penny Post-age, by a public meeting here last evening, and am now fairly in the field. I hope to be able to address four or five meetings a week on the subject, and get two or three hundred petitions sent up to Congress during the next two months. I am also writing a short article for some newspaper every day on the subject, and send one today to the National Intelligencer.

Now would it not be best to fix upon the middle of March for bringing the motion before the House? This would give us time to pour in a stream of petitions,—say two or three a day, and thus prepare the way. I have offered, in all the articles I have sent to the papers, to forward *manuscript* forms of a petition all ready for signatures, to those who would engage to get them filled out and sent up to Congress. I have received many applications already.

I think I shall try to get a hearing at the state legisla-tures, and induce them to memorialize in behalf of the boon. Am now on the way to Boston, and hope that a meeting may be got up there in Faneuil Hall, with Abbott Law-rence [12] in the chair. After this I intend to visit New York and Philadelphia, but think I had better defer my visit to Washington, until about the time the motion is brought forward.

Now we must look to you to champion this enterprise in Congress. I expect to be in Boston for a week, and should be very glad to receive at least a few lines from you, directed

[12] Abbott Lawrence (1792-1855), merchant, manufacturer, diplomat, states-man and philanthropist. Burritt recorded in his *Diary*, under the date Jan 1, 1856, that Lawrence did not believe in the emancipation of the slaves, who, he thought, were too degraded for freedom.

to the Post Office there, stating whether you approve my program of operations.

Yours Truly,

Elihu Burritt

SUMNER MSS., *Letters Received*, Vol. XXII
Harvard College Library

Boston
Marlboro House
Dec. 14, 1853

Dear Mr Sumner

I have been in Boston about a week preparing for the great meeting in Faneuil Hall on Ocean Penny Postage, which is to come off on Thursday evening, the 22nd. The mayor is to preside, and I hope many of the leading men of the city will take an active part in the proceedings. How I wish it could have been held before you left, that you might have been present to say one of your grand words for the system!

Could you not write a dozen words which might be read on the occasion? I would [not] suggest anything which might be a tax on your time, but if you could send a few lines, they would be a valuable contribution to the demonstration. I hope the *petitions* are beginning to flow into congress. When I have done here, I intend to visit the principal towns, and present the subject, get up petitions etc. If you would fix upon the middle or end of March for bringing forward the motion, before that time we shall bring an avalanche of public opinion upon congress in favour of the measure. Perhaps you will be disposed to address a few lines to me for the meeting, directed simply to Boston.

Yours Truly & Ever,

Elihu Burritt

SUMNER MSS., *Letters Received*, Vol. XXII
Harvard College Library

Boston, Dec. 15, 1853

[To Gerrit Smith]

My dear Sir

From my heart I thank you earnestly for your good and generous gift to the Ocean Penny Postage cause and to myself. I gratefully accept it, and will appropriate it as you request. I have come on here to *agitate* for this movement. We are to have a grand public meeting in Faneuil Hall on Thursday evening of next week, the mayor in the chair, and expect a large and impressive demonstration to open the campaign with. I intend then to visit different towns, and present the subject, get up petitions.

I feel the deepest concern for your health, and pray you to be very careful of this precious gift, for your life and labours in Congress are full of hope to human freedom in this country.

Yours ever truly,

Elihu Burritt.

MS. MISCELLANEOUS COLLECTIONS
Massachusetts Historical Society

New Britain, Conn.
Jan. 3, 1854

My dear Mr Sumner

We have fairly launched the Ocean Penny Postage movement under favourable auspices. The meeting in Faneuil Hall was very satisfactory and effective. Next Friday I am to speak to a public meeting in the Broadway Tabernacle, New York, and next week I hope we may have a grand meeting in Philadelphia. I thank you most sincerely for your noble and excellent letter. Every word told with great effect. It contained a whole argument. I hope you have seen some notice of the meeting. I am trying to agitate through the press, and to send off an article every day to some journal, when I am in any fixed place. I hope petitions are being presented in Congress; and that they will continue to flow in steadily for weeks. I hope you may be able to bring forward the subject in a formal motion about the end of March. I intend to go on to Washington about the middle of that month, to make a little interest for the subject among the members.

Yours Ever & Truly
Elihu Burritt

New York, Feb. 13, 1854

My dear Charles Sumner

I am now on my way to Washington, where I expect to arrive on Saturday next; not to *lobby* with the members of Congress now in behalf of Ocean Penny Postage, but to see you for half an hour, and to get a few notes of introduction from Southern members to gentlemen in the South. For I am now on a long tour through the Southern and Western states, expecting to go as far as New Orleans, thence up the Mississippi into the Great West, then to return to Washington about the 1st of April, when I hope you will be able to bring the question before Congress in a practical shape. By that time, I trust, the Nebraska Bill will have been assigned to the toomb of the Capulets. How much I should like to hear you speak on that question!

I hope I may have an opportunity of speaking to a public meeting on Ocean Penny Postage in Washington. I have recently addressed the members of the legislatures of Massachusetts & Rhode Island on the subject, and tomorrow am to speak to that of New Jersey. Hope the resolutions and memorials of these legislatures will reach Congress.

Hoping to see you soon,

I am Ever Yours
Elihu Burritt

[MS. JOURNALS]

[Washington] Thursday, March 9 [1854]

Immediately after breakfast called upon General Rusk [13] who received me with the greatest cordiality. He was smoking a pipe, free and easy & natural. He said he had read my tract, and went with me in its conclusions. He was in favour of a two cent rate for the ocean transit, and would try to get the Committee to report in favour of it. He saw the benefit that would be conferred upon the emigrants by it. Unfortunately the present Post Office Administration were opposed even to the cheap inland postage. He had endeavored to reduce it to *two cents*, but had been thwarted. I urged upon him the importance of inducing the P. M. General to recognize our inland rate as applying also to all letters that cross the ocean. He asked me for a copy of my O. P. P. placard, and I gave him several copies of the new tract for distribution among the Postal Committee. He was very affable & kind, and asked me to call again. I felt this was a most satisfactory result. Called on Mr King at the P. O. Department, and had a talk with him about the new arrangement for transmitting the mails to Australia. He said he had urged the P. M. Gen. not to charge anything more than our usual inland rate on the letters sent by the new line of packets to that country; so that the whole charge shall only be 5 cents. This would be a complete adoption of the Ocean Penny Postage plan on one of the longest routes on the globe. I next went up to the Capitol where Mr Clubb [?] introduced me to Mr Benson,[14] of Maine, who had a resolution on his table, ready to offer for O. P. P. He introduced me to full twenty M. C.'s from different parts of the country, all of whom were exceedingly courte-

[13] Thomas Jefferson Rusk (1803-1857), a native of South Carolina, took an active part in the Texan Revolution, and served as senator from Texas from its admission as a state into the Union until his death in 1857.

[14] Samuel Page Benson (1804-1876), elected to the Thirty-third Congress as a Whig and as a Republican to the Thirty-fourth Congress.

ous and complimentary. I was surprised to find them so well acquainted with my operations. I gave them all a tract, which they promised to read. Also wrote down a few points for Mr Benson. Returned to my room and wrote a pretty long article for the Intelligencer and another one for the Sentinel. Called upon Mr Fenton of the former, who was right hearty in the cause. Talked with him a long while. He said he would insert the article in the morning paper. This was a good day's progress.

Monday, March 20 [1854]

This was truly a long day of labour. Sent off an article to the Advertiser, Kingston, Jamaica. Wrote before breakfast twenty notes to editors to go with the tracts. After breakfast, called upon Gen. Rusk, and asked him if he would report the Bill which I had drawn up with Mr Kings assistance for Ocean Penny Postage. He looked at it, and said without hesitation that he would adopt it and bring in a report in its favor. He went for the whole principle involved in it. It might be a week or two before he could bring it forward. He would recommend it to the Committee and should like to have me meet them sometime. He was cordial, frank, and fully up to the proposition in all its fulness. . . .

Friday, April 7. [1854]

Wrote notes to editors after breakfast. . . . . Spent the afternoon in getting one of the placards on O. P. P. put up in the Rotunda of the Capitol

[Richmond, Va.] Saturday, May 20 [1854]

. . . While waiting at the hotel . . . . another gentleman introduced himself to me as a member of the Mechanics Association before which I lectured here in 1841. He said the Society soon run down, with plenty of funds in its treasury; that the employers and manufacturers were rather adverse to the acquisition of knowledge by their young men and apprentices, lest it should raise them above their condition as laborers, as labor was regarded as belonging chiefly to the negroes. He said there was only one public school in the city, though it contained a population of 35,000; that it was difficult to establish free schools even in large towns; and quite impracticable in the country. . . .

New Britain, Conn.
July 5, 1854

Dear Sumner,

I have finished my long tour in the South and West, and am again at home, in my native town. My journey has been, in every way, very satisfactory and successful. Although I and many of my friends apprehended a rough reception for me in the South, I was treated with great kindness and courtesy by all I met, and the cheap ocean postage scheme was received with the liveliest sympathy. I called upon editors, lawyers, bankers and leading merchants, and all signed petitions with hearty good will. You have noticed, doubtless, that Sir Fogey Badger, Butler, Evans, Bell [15] & other Southern senators have presented petitions from the principal towns of their native States. I now intend to remain here for a few weeks, and then to leave for England. I should be exceedingly glad to carry back with me some evidence that the measure had made one good step in Congress.

If Gen. Rusk would but give notice of his bill, and ask for the printing of his report, it would be a most encouraging beginning. I could then take copies of it with me to England, to distribute among the M Ps and such a document would have much weight. If you would just give the General a social jog in this direction, he might effect this preliminary step this session, and the discussion of the subject might go over to the next. It would meet my best ex-

[15] George E. Badger (1795-1866), senator from North Carolina 1846-1855; Andrew Pickens Butler (1796-1857), senator from South Carolina 1846-1857; Josiah James Evans (1786-1858), senator from South Carolina 1853-1858; John Bell (1797-1869), senator from Tennessee 1847-1859.

pectation, if the Report were merely printed this session on the authority of the Senate.

And now I want to thank you with my whole heart for your grand and brave rejoinder to Butler [16] and Mason.[17] It was the best, bravest thing done in the Senate this many a year.

I think more hearts in the free states will glory in your courageous and overwhelming reply to the plantation senators, than in any public effort of your life. You must have made it on short notice. I never read anything with more satisfaction than your reference to Mason. *Entre nous*, the Everett Whigs of Massachusetts must have inwardly rejoiced that the task of castigating those Southern braggarts devolved upon you instead of him.

Yours faithfully and ever,
Elihu Burritt

SUMNER MSS., *Letters Received*, Vol. XXV
Harvard College Library

New Britain Conn. July 29, 1854

Dear Sumner—

Next Wednesday I sail for England from Boston. I intend to find one of your portraits in B[oston] to take with me to England, as "a counterfeit Presentment" of the man. I shall remember that commission *de coeur* and hope I may succeed to your innermost satisfaction. I suppose you will soon be released for a while from the arduous service of the senatorial camp, to rest & reinvigorate in these northern latitudes. You have acted a grand Roman role in the Senate, and you will have a reception at the North from all parties which will be gratifying.

I suppose that it is doubtful whether Senator Rusk will bring forward his report this session, it is now so late. But

[16] Andrew Pickens Butler (1796-1857), proslavery senator from South Carolina.
[17] John Young Mason (1799-1859), Democrat and proslavery senator from Virginia.

I hope in the next it will come up for discussion. I received a few lines from him the other day, saying that he intended to bring it in as an amendment to Old's bill.[18] If that bill should come before the Senate this session, I hope it will receive its everlasting *quietus*. If you will occasionally advert to the subject when conversing with Gen. Rusk, it will keep it alive in his mind, and stimulate him to action. It would be a great step—almost a triumph, if the General's report could be printed this session. But if it should go over to another, I trust he will not lose it in the interval.

And now, for awhile, *adieu!*

Yours faithfully & Ever

Elihu Burritt

SUMNER MSS., *Letters Received*, Vol. XXV
Harvard College Library

New Britain, Conn.
July 29, 1854

Hon Gerrit Smith, Esq. M. C.
My dear Friend

I am now about to sail for England, and write a few lines to say how much I wish the best blessing of God may rest upon you for all your noble words and works for His glory and the good of man. I wish most earnestly that God and humanity might own you entirely, and employ all those great gifts with which you have been endowed—that you might devote yourself to public life and labor, without feeling compelled or burdened by the pressure of private business.

You have done a great work in one session. The influence you have exerted has been most successful and capital, especially upon Southern members. I honestly think that by your social intercourse with these Southern members, you have produced an impression of inestimable value,

[18] Edson B. Olds (1802-1869), Democratic representative from Ohio.

which will work for years in the best direction. When you have spent a year or two in comparative retirement, I hope you will be sent up to the Senate from New York.

As soon as this Ocean Penny Postage reform is carried, I hope to give myself to a considerable extent to colonizing *Free Labor* in the Slave States. I shall be glad to write to you occasionally from London, and hope you will see the *Bond* regularly. . . . [MS. cut off]
MS. COLLECTIONS
Massachusetts Historical Society

35 Broad Street Buildings
London
Dec. 6, 1854

My dear Sumner,

I suppose you are again in the midst of the struggle for freedom and right, and are daily confronting the champions of slavery in the Senate. How rapidly has passed the recess of Congress! I have read your great words at Worcester with greatest pleasure. I suppose you have kept "posted up" in regard to affairs on this side of the Atlantic. Have you read John Bright's glorious, heroic letter? [10] You will receive with this a copy, with the "Blue Book" authorities corroborating his statements. Is it not grand in him to face and breast the tide of public opinion as he has done? England needs more of such men. No people in the world have been more frequently and fatally deluded and victimized by their *press* than the English nation. I earnestly hope our country may some day be emancipated from the domination of the British press; that we shall be able to form estimates of other nations that shall be impartial & truthful, and not after the proud, pigheaded prejudices engendered by British editors.

And, now, as this is to be a short session of Congress, I

[10] *The Public Letters of the Right Hon. John Bright, M. P.*, collected and edited by H. J. Leech (London, 1855), pp. 26-36.

write more especially to express the hope that you will put up General Rusk to move early in the *Cheap Ocean Postage* question. You remember that I wrote a *Report* for him, which he approved, and I trust he will bring it forward early.

If you will remind him of the matter occasionally it will serve to stir him up to action. Let me beg you to associate this great and beneficent reform with your name & senatorial career. I am sure you could carry it through with a short speech; that several senators of various *couleurs* will support you. I received a letter from Mr Upham [29] of the House, soon after my return to England; and he seemed to be quite earnest in the matter, and ready to move at the right opportunity. I write a few lines to Senator Rusk by this steamer, and enclose them in this, and beg you to let it be dropped in the post for him. I leave it with you, hoping some issue may be obtained during the present session of Congress, which shall be gratifying to all the friends of the movement. I am to edit a little monthly magazine, called *"The Citizen of the World,"* which I have directed to be sent to you from Philadelphia. I hope you may occasionally glance at the leading article, as I intend to say a bold and truthful word about European affairs; which may not always accord with the views of the people of the United States.

And read the letter of John Bright, which you will receive forthwith. Excuse me for asking you to see posted so many little notes as I intend to enclose in this. It is an illustration of the necessity of Ocean Penny Postage.

Ever & faithfully yours,

Elihu Burritt

SUMNER MSS., *Letters Received*, Vol. XXVIII
Harvard College Library

---

[29] Charles Wentworth Upham (1802-1875), Whig representative from Salem, Massachusetts.

New Britain, Conn. Jan 11, 1856

Dear Sumner,

I thank you heartily for your letter: I had intended to have written myself long ere this; but, knowing you were out of Boston a good deal, I waited until you should be settled down in Washington. I heard Mr Richard speak of bringing out your orations, but I know not how far he had proceeded with the work before I left England. I will write him a letter on the subject, and let you know how it stands at present. I am sure a collection of your speeches would have a large reading in England, and all I can do to assist in bringing them out shall be done with great pleasure—I hope you have a good fund of strength for the great struggle that must come on in Congress, in behalf of freedom. You must be glad to have such a band of strong, *backbone* men to stand by you. I shall read your words uttered in the Senate with great interest.

I hope an opportunity will occur this session for bringing forward the Cheap Ocean Postage question. The Collins Monopoly and the Franking system are two great obstacles to this postal reform; but I hope they may be overcome.

I wrote to General Rusk, expressing the hope that he would still interest himself in the matter. You know I wrote a *Report* for him, which I hope may be available, when the time comes. Will you not occasionally touch him up on the question? I have never received any acknowledgment of my letter; but think he must have received it.

I am putting a new "iron in the fire"—Immediate and National Emancipation by Compensation, devoting all the Public lands west of the Mississippi to the object. Intend soon to take the field and send in petitions to the end.

Yours Ever & faithfully

Elihu Burritt

New Britain, Ct.
Feb. 13, 1856

Dear Charles Sumner,

I am rejoiced indeed that you have moved so efficiently in bringing up the Cheap Penny Postage question. Will not the committee now be constrained to *report* on the matter, and will not Gen. Rusk be willing to present the report I drew up for him? I ardently hope he will. Can I do anything to help you in this work? Will you not make a speech on the report of the Committee when it comes up? I have one more campaign of lectures to make, then I shall be on hand in getting up O P P Petitions. I intend to spend a few weeks in Washington in April. I send you one of my little "Year Books" [21] and hope it may be useful to you. Will you not glance at a few of the first pages?

Ever & faithfully yours,
Elihu Burritt

SUMNER MSS., *Letters Received*, Vol. XXIX
Harvard College Library

[21] *Year Book of the Nations* (New York, 1856). This was a statistical abstract of war expenditures by different nations.

CHAPTER IV

SLAVERY AND CIVIL WAR

BURRITT'S activity in behalf of international peace and cheap ocean postage slackened only because of the growing acuteness of the slavery problem in his native land. Although it is almost certain that he had opposed slavery from his earliest youth,[1] it was not until 1845 that he began actively to work for abolition. In that year he became interested in the movement for the production of cotton by free labor. This idea, which was particularly dear to the Quakers, was being promoted by two Philadelphia Friends, George Taylor and Samuel Rhodes, and by Joseph Sturge in England.[2] Burritt persuaded the League of Universal Brotherhood to add this cause to its program, and in addition supported the North American Free Labor Produce Association.

Burritt had some hope that the successful production of cotton in the South by free labor would convince slaveowners that the idea was practicable. He looked with favor on the payment of premiums to Southern farmers for the largest cotton yield grown without slave labor. He did what he could to promote the migration of German and English farmers to the South to swell the ranks of nonslave producers of cotton, and he helped

---

[1] His brother Elijah had, when Elihu was a child, made great sacrifices for his abolitionist principles during his residence in Georgia; he was finally forced to flee for his life in the middle of the night when a hostile mob attacked his dwelling

[2] *The British Friend*, Vol III (7th Month, 1845), p 108 Lewis Tappan was also sympathetic. Burritt's MS. *Journal*, Feb. 11, 1854.

promote the project of building a factory devoted solely to the manufacture of cotton which had never been touched by a slave. In Birmingham and Manchester Burritt helped establish experimental shops in which only such cotton cloth was sold.

The most striking arguments of the learned blacksmith for this scheme were those addressed to wage laborers. He insisted that slavery degraded free workers by forcing them to compete with chattel slaves. It was increasingly felt by Northern capitalists, he pointed out, that "the condition of slavery must, somehow, be accepted as the base line, the point of departure of their operations; that, somehow, it must determine the compensation and honor of free labor. Slavery is to be the base line on which the economist is to plant one foot of his compasses, and, with the other, step off a thin parallel, on which *free* men work for six pence a day, and live on raw turnips or a handful of rice." [3]

As the crisis became more acute, Burritt saw the necessity of more immediate and drastic action than the free labor project. He shared the views of the left-wing abolitionists, led by Garrison, that the North was equally guilty with the South for the sin of slavery. Like Garrison, he was too much imbued with the doctrine of non-resistance to look with favor on schemes to incite the slaves to insurrection, or to provoke civil war for the freedom of the blacks. At the same time his residence in England had familiarized him with the successful emancipation of slaves in the British West Indies by national compensation of the planters. This scheme, he thought, was the most feasible program for antislavery men in America: it might rally the support of the more moder-

[3] *Bond of Brotherhood*, new series, no. 51, Oct., 1854.

ate slaveowners, and thus prevent civil war.[4] He proposed the use of the revenue from the sale of the vast unoccupied lands of the West as the means of effecting the compensation,[5] and also urged the necessity of governmental assistance in the education of the emancipated blacks.[6] From 1856 to the eve of the Civil War Burritt devoted all his time and strength to this plan.

To further the idea of compensated emancipation, Burritt edited a periodical, *North and South*. He wrote the editorials in his shirt sleeves, on the head of a lime cask in his barn—"pen and hoe alternating through the day." In addition he personally carried the gospel up and down the land. One winter, a typical one, he journeyed 10,000 miles, speaking in the largest cities as well as in smaller towns. His *Journal* records the receptions he had, and the progress of the movement. In addition to almost incessant lectures, he conducted an enormous correspondence: in one month he wrote five hundred letters to enlist support. Finally, in August, 1856, Burritt organized a convention at Cleveland, from which a formal organization resulted. The convention at Cleveland was attended by many well-known men, including Gerrit Smith, member of Congress and a distinguished abolitionist, Mark Hopkins, president of Williams College, Dr. Eliphalet Nott, Governor Fairchild of Vermont, and others. Emerson, who wholeheartedly supported the movement, was unable to attend the convention.[7]

[4] Burritt wrote his first article on compensated emancipation on Nov. 27, 1855. MS. *Journal*, Nov. 27, 1855.

[5] Burritt somewhat inconsistently favored the free homestead bill. MS. *Journal*, Apr. 19, 1854.

[6] Elihu Burritt, *A Plan of Brotherly Co-Partnership of the North and South* (N. Y., 1856).

[7] The best printed account of this movement is to be found in *The Bond of Brotherhood*, new series, 1856-1859.

Although there was much support, Burritt was unable to commit a major political party to adopt the scheme. The new Republican party drew much of its support from Western farmers who, because of their desire to have the public domain given freely to settlers, could not favor a plan which was based on the idea of selling the unoccupied regions. It is true that Lincoln[3] was attracted by the idea of compensated emancipation, which he later recommended to the loyal border states.

But Burritt could not carry the country: he felt that the hysteria which resulted in the South from the John Brown raid closed all avenues to any discussion of a peaceful settlement of the slavery controversy.

Until the very outbreak of hostilities Burritt hoped, however, that by some miracle war might be prevented. Consequently he rejoiced that the authorities at Washington took so conciliatory a position and he welcomed every suggestion for compromise that was not an out and out surrender to the slavocracy. When at last blood was shed, Burritt agreed with Horace Greeley, editor of the *New York Tribune,* that it would have been well to let the erring sisters depart in peace. Although he loved the Union he loved peace more; he would rather sacrifice the principle of national unity than see his fellow Americans embark on a cruel and bloody civil war.

The learned blacksmith differed from the vast majority of the organized friends of peace when he refused to compromise with his conscience and resolutely held out against the argument that this war was merely a domes-

[3] It is quite possible that Lincoln became interested in this idea as a result of two lectures which Burritt made at Springfield, Illinois, in 1856 and 1857. On both occasions he was cordially received by Gen William Herndon, Lincoln's law partner. Burritt, MS. *Journal,* June 26, 1856, and Jan. 7, 1857

tic insurrection which federal authority must legitimate-
ly crush. With a mere handful of other pacifists he insisted that the struggle *was* a war, to be opposed like any
other war. It required great courage as well as remarkable consistency to maintain this position, for there was
tremendous pressure on idealists to accept the war on the
assumption that it would result in the freedom of the
slave. Yet Burritt did not falter. For a time he even
considered taking part in some end-the-war movement,
but he confined himself to open criticism.

From the first Burritt had predicted, indeed, that as
an incidental result of the war the slave would win his
freedom. He thought that the South, once the pinch of
defeat was keenly felt, would itself emancipate its slaves
in order to enlist them as soldiers for the cause of independence. And Burritt, feeling that the Negroes would
subsequently be treated far better if they achieved their
freedom at the hands of their former masters than they
would if Northern soldiers broke their chains, hoped that
the Confederacy would proclaim emancipation.

Burritt's zeal for freedom was, of course, so great that
he rejoiced when President Lincoln issued his proclamation of emancipation. He took great delight in the fact
that as the Northern armies pushed southward into the
Confederacy the freed Negro was established on small
farms and encouraged to cultivate cotton: this, he felt,
was a vindication of his own early enthusiasm for free
labor production. Once the war was over Burritt did
what he could to favor the idea that the freed man must
be provided with the means of education, and that both
his Northern and English friends must bend all their
efforts to work for the dissolution of prejudice against
him, and for his political and social equality.

[MS. JOURNALS]

[Andover, Mass.] Saturday, Jan. 21 [1854]

Had a long talk with Harriet B. Stowe [9] on my proposition to make a trial of the cultivation of cotton in the Southern States by free labour. She fully approves of the plan, and offers to assist in carrying it out. She encourages me to make a tour through the Slave States, talk with the planters, and get as much information as I can, especially upon the inter-state slave-trade, upon which she wishes to write a book. She offered to contribute to my expenses even. She entered into my other operations, and promised to write on them, in her book of travels in Europe which is to appear soon. . . I left at 2 for Amesbury, where I arrived about 5. Went directly to the house of John G. Whittier, the grand and noble poet of humanity. He met me at the door and gave me a good and brotherly welcome. . . . We had a long conversation on the past, present and future, and upon passages of our mutual life.

"Uncle Toms Cabin"
Andover, Mass.
Jan. 21, 1854.

John Ecroyd Esq.,[10]
My dear Sir,

I am now writing under the roof of Harriet Beecher Stowe, with whom I have had a long conversation on the subject of growing cotton by free labour in the Southern States. She heartily commends the project, and offers to assist in carrying it out. I think we can raise money enough to try the experiment on a small scale to begin with. But it is of vast importance to have the right man to head the en-

[9] Burritt had called upon Mrs. Stowe in England. For Mrs. Stowe's impressions of the learned blacksmith, see Charles Edward Stowe, *Life of Harriet Beecher Stowe* (Boston and New York, 1890), pp 223-224.

[10] John Ecroyd was a Friend of Bradford, Yorkshire, engaged in the textile business. He did not accept Burritt's invitation.

terprise. I am confident that you are the best fitted by experience and principle for this post, and I now write to ask if you would be willing to undertake to manage a small plantation of 100 or 200 acres in South Carolina, Georgia or Alabama, and on what terms? We are confident that a successful experiment, even on a small scale, would be frought with great and important consequences just at this moment, and I know you would enter into the work with a devotion and heart interest which few would bring into it. Such qualities as you possess are indispensably necessary to the success of the experiment. For want of free coloured labour at first, I have thought a few stalwart Germans fresh from the Continent might be the best hands we could find. They might be found in any number in New York. I think such labourers would be less likely to excite suspicion as "abolitionist agitators" in the south than any other class attainable. But these arrangements must be determined after your arrival. I write now to ask if you can come over to the United States by the 1st. of *March*, so as to be able to commence the experiment this forthcoming season? I would go with you into the Southern States and we would select a farm or plantation in some healthy locality, susceptible of the cultivation of the best kind of cotton. I think we could make the conditions satisfactory to you. I will not enlarge upon them now, but merely ask you to say, if possible, by return steamer, if you could head this enterprise, provided these conditions were perfectly satisfactory? And whether you could possibly reach America by the 1st. March?

I expect to be in Washington about that time, and propose to make a tour through South Carolina, Georgia and Alabama, etc. for the purpose of exploring out the capacities of the soil for Free Labour production. If you would join me at Washington, we would go together, and select a farm, which should be bought and stocked with free labour, implements etc. for you, and which you should cultivate on such conditions as should be perfectly satisfactory to you. I fear we cannot exchange more than one letter before the time arrives at which it would be necessary to leave England for America, but if you will write per return steamer to say you will come, immediately or by the 1st. March, we will guarantee you against any loss.

I am sorry that I could not write before on this subject, but it was necessary to have a good deal of conference with friends in various parts of the country, and I think the project has now reached a stage at which you would safely embark in it without even waiting for much correspondence.

I beg you to write me per return steamer, so that we may be guided in our future operations by your decision.

Please direct to me in New Britain, Connecticut, U. S. A.

Yours truly,

Elihu Burritt

MS. COLLECTIONS
Friends House

[MS. JOURNALS]

[Wilmington, N. C.] Thursday, May 24, [1854]

. . . While walking up the Main Street I saw by sheer accident a slave sold at auction. As I stepped up to the crowd, I thought that the chattel was a pair of horses, or a carriage, and looked about for one of these objects; when, just as the hammer fell, I saw that it was a man; and I turned away with a cold chill of horror. It was the first time I had ever witnessed the spectacle; I hope it may be the last.

[London] Monday, October 30 [1854]

Commenced writing a paper on extending the Premium System for stimulating the production of Cotton to the British Empire. Hope the Manchester Chamber of Commerce will allow me to read it before their body at one of their meetings. If they would take up the plan they would carry it through with good power and success . . .

Tuesday, Oct. 31 [1854]

. . . . I spoke to him [Richard Cobden] of the plan of stimulating the production of cotton by *Premiums,* and he approved my idea of presenting the subject to the Manchester Chamber of Commerce but thought it might be opposed to their views of Free Trade. It was truly a pleasant evening.

Wednesday, Feb. 28 [1855]

The last day of winter. It has been a cold season, and a vast amount of suffering and misery has been experienced by the poor. Farm-labor has been suspended, and manufacturing industry greatly cramped, especially by the war. There has been a great Bread Riot in Liverpool, and there is the most pinching poverty in every town.

I trust that the people will learn some valuable lessons from this experience; that they will feel it deeply what war costs them, and how they have been deluded by its cruelties.

Saturday March 24 [1855]

Wrote for the Bond in the forenoon. Called upon Mr George Peabody,[11] of whom I had asked an interview some evening, for the purpose of trying to enlist him in the Free Labor Cotton System. He was very kind, and took me about his great establishment and introduced me to his new partner, Mr Morgan [12] from Boston who married John Pierpont's daughter. Hope to make a more intimate acquaintance with the Americans in London and to obtain their cooperation in some of our movements, especially in the Free Labor.

[11] George Peabody (1795–1869), American merchant, financier and philanthropist, resided in London
[12] Junius Spencer Morgan (1813–1890), international banker.

Wednesday, April 4 [1855]

. . Made a little progress on an article for the second leader [of the *Citizen*] entitled "*The Free Labor Principle*" in the Slave States. Propose to show that the planters pay more for *Slave* labor than is paid for the best *free* employed in agriculture in Europe; that they get the *worst* labor in the world, because it is *hopeless*; that they then endeavor to raise its character and value by infusing *hope* into it which they endeavor to do by giving the slaves piece-work, and paying them for what they perform over their daily tasks. . . .

35 Broad Street Buildings, London
July 21, 1855

[To Gerrit Smith]

My dear Friend,

I hope you are quite well and hopeful in regard to "*the good time coming.*" I see you moving frequently in the journals in the form of letters, speeches, etc. You are almost the only Abolitionist in America with whom I fully agree on all points. I shall never forget your speech on the Nebraska Bill, when you denied the right of slavery to exist on one foot of our broad land. That is my doctrine. As for the watchword *no Slavery* outside the *Slave States*, it sounds small and almost cowardly to my ears. No slavery inside any State, say you and I, and thousands, I hope. I suppose you are as much absorbed as ever with your flood of business. Hope however you get time to glance at papers you receive. I wonder if you see my *Citizen of the World*, published in Philadelphia? If so, I hope you sometimes glance at the leading articles, and that you approve their spirit generally. You will see that I have ventured to diverge from the popular views in reference to certain questions. I now expect to return to America early in the fall to spend the winter, when I hope to see you in your home, where I have never yet met you. I shall be so glad to talk over plans with you, and feel myself somewhat in co-partnership with you in carrying them out. . . .

And now with every good wish,

I am ever faithfully yours,

Elihu Burritt

MS. COLLECTIONS
Massachusetts Historical Society

[MS. JOURNALS]

Monday July 30 [1855]

. . . In the evening went to J. B. Gough's [13] Farewell Meeting. Exeter Hall was densely crowded before the proceedings began. Several addresses were presented to Gough, full of the warmest praise and good wishes. He made a most eloquent and thrilling oration. Some of his figures and passages were overpowering. His farewell affected many to tears.

Thursday, Nov. 8 [1855]

. . . Received a note from Wm Goodell, saying I was elected a Vice-President of the Radical Abolitionist Party. This is rather embarrassing for me, and I fear it may interpose an obstacle to my Free Labor operations in the South, if I accept the appointment, on one hand, and offend them if I decline. I shall write them a brief statement of my situation, hoping they will not press me to accept the post.

[New Britain] Thursday, May 15 [1856]

My head was very heavy, and I feared complete prostration. Paid $1.50 for the handbills, which took every dollar of my own money. Thus, instead of earning anything by my lecture, I have lost about $7, and two days. Mary lent me $5 to enable me to get home and pay the hire of the horse and carriage. Returned to New Britain and went to work im-

---

[13] John B. Gough (1817-1886), famous lecturer on temperance. See his *Autobiography and Personal Recollections* (Springfield, Mass., 1870).

mediately on the hill. Feel that my literary labors are drawing to a close, and that I must now depend more upon the labor of my hands for a support.

Monday, June 2 [1856]

Working on the hill all day, and with the assistance of an Irishman finished planting the little patch of corn, which will constitute the head and front of my grain growing for this year. Feel lame and sore about the side & back, owing to holding plough for two days, and wrestling with turf & stones. The National Democratic Convention meets today to nominate candidates for the Presidency. Pierce, Douglas & Buchanan are the rival ones. . .

35 Broad Street Buildings, London
Oct 6, 1856

[To Gerrit Smith]

My Dear Friend,

I am again at my old post and duties in London, and venture to send you a few lines to say that I remember you with increased sentiments of affectionate esteem. And you have again entered upon the retirement of private life. What a chapter of deep interest must this congressional campaign have been in your life! I have watched your course with the greatest satisfaction in Congress. I believe you performed a great mission there, and exerted an influence for good which will last for years. You have more fully spoken my sentiments there than anyone in either house. I have read your letters in Douglass Paper with complete sympathy. I like your position in reference to *Cuba*, although it may not be *politic* in the modern sense— in the sense a le du compromise—to take this ground. I believe in two cardinal points in reference to human civilization—No. 1. No man can hold property in *Man*. No. 2 No Government can hold property in a *people*. I think you and I are one in that belief. How I should like to talk with you on these subjects!—Will you kindly read that article in the Oct. Bond, entitled "Onward! Onward!" in which I have proposed to double our operations on the Continent. I hope the American ladies will lend a hand to this special enterprise. I wish you would call Mrs. Smith's attention to it. Perhaps she and Mrs. Miller and a few other ladies in Peterboro would undertake to raise about $15, which would defray the expense of publishing an Olive Leaf in a Continental journal for *6 months*. This would be a great help. I would send to them monthly a copy of the journal containing the Olive Leaf for which they paid, that they might see the *modus operandi*, the very sewing machine employed by them in scattering these holy seed-truths among the nations. I have already arranged for the publication of the *Olive Leaf* in *six* new journals on the Continent, to be supported by the few ladies societies in America. Although there is no such circle in Peterboro, still if Mrs. Smith and a few ladies there would undertake to raise $15, it would support a seed-sower in the field for six months.

I am trying to launch another antislavery enterprise to be worked simultaneously with that system of *Premiums* to which you subscribed. I am endeavoring to form Free Labour *Farming* colonies to be planned in the very heart of the Slave States, to grow cotton by Free Labour. This will be an exceedingly difficult and delicate matter, but I am enjoying it, *sink or swim*. I wish you could exchange some of your wild land for about 500 acres of the same quality in Georgia. I would endeavor to plant twenty vigorous freemen upon it from England, Scotland or Germany in the course of a year.

Do write a few lines at least. My heart yearns to be in fellowship with you, and to *guest* itself in your happy home.

Affectionately, Ever Yours

Elihu Burritt

MS. MISCELLANEOUS COLLECTIONS
Massachusetts Historical Society

[MS. JOURNALS]

[Rochester] Tuesday Nov. 11 [1856]

Went on to Rochester, and delivered my lecture before the Ladies Anti-Slavery Society; Fred Douglass [14] in the chair. They listened attentively until the close, and I spoke with great earnestness. But when I sat down, up sprang Dr Porter and denounced my compensated scheme with great and almost bitter energy. A Mr Bloss followed in the same spirit; then Fred Douglass gave his testimony against me, but in a courteous way. I did not undertake to reply, but merely asked him to take "a show of hands," when a majority of the meeting agreed with the proposition.

[Northampton] Tuesday, Feb. 10 [1857]

Arranged to get some one to get hay for the cattle, and take them back to the barn as soon as possible. Then set out on my second western trip. My first attempt was in Northampton. The weather was cold, the wind was high, and walking slippery. I did not expect many persons, and my expectations were disappointed on the wrong side. Only about 15 persons came in—too few to address in a formal lecture so I just talked with them about half an hour on the scheme of Compensated Emancipation. One or two made a few remarks, but I had the conversation to myself. Lost here about $7 in all.

Pittsfield, Mass., Feb. 13, 1857

[To Gerrit Smith]

My dear Friend,

How I long to see you and talk over the new phases of the present and future! I have just returned from a long tour in the Western States, touching St. Louis, Iowa City, & Milwaukee, as the bounding points of the journey. Everywhere *Compensated Emancipation* has been well received, by

[14] Frederick Douglass (1817-1895), Negro abolitionist who escaped from slavery, lecturer, author and, after the Civil War, United States minister to Haiti.

all parties. I feel more sanguine than ever in the power and practicality of the idea. I am now on my way westward again to finish off States that I could not thoroughly visit on my last trip. I expect to spend the Sabbath in Lockport. Will you not drop me a line directed to Buffalo, where I am to be on Tuesday night. Say if you have not time to glance at my little pamphlet I sent you, developing the Emancipation scheme? I feel anxious on this trip to enlist materials for a national convention, such as we spoke of. Let us fix upon a point for it. I am inclined to think that we had better let the *West* take the *apparent* lead in the matter. They constitute a kind of middle ground between the North and the South. Besides, the subject has been presented more fully in the West. Suppose we take four points and select one of them at a later date, or even now. The one *you* prefer, must be the one.

Cincinnati, Cleveland, Chicago, Buffalo. I rather lean to *Cleveland*, because that city has never been the scene of a great national political convention. Cincinnati has too much of the *Democratic* platform reputation.

How long does a *call* for such a convention need to be? Would it not be best that it should be *concise* and very brief? inviting all those willing to extinguish Slavery by National Compensation? Something that one could insert in the *Tribune*, *Times* or *Herald* as an advertisment. Need it be more than ten lines in length? Do write me at once on these points.

Faithfully & Ever Yours
Elihu Burritt

MS. MISCELLANEOUS COLLECTIONS
Massachusetts Historical Society

[MS. JOURNALS]

[Adrian, Mich.] Friday, Feb. 27 [1857]

Mr Angier [at Toledo] would make me his guest and receive nothing for my stay with him. Commenced an article for the *London Star*,[15] and hope to write one weekly in the shape of *American Correspondence*, with the view of earning something. My prospects pecuniarily are rather unpromising, as my lectures yield but little over expenses. Went on to Adrian, in Michigan.

The evening was very unfavorable, besides being preoccupied by a Fireman's Ball. Still there were about 125 present, most of whom listened with great attention. Think a few adherents to the plan were gained. The editor of the Democratic paper seemed quite favorable to it. Receipts about $18 against $11 expenditure.

New Britain, Conn., July 21, 1857

Rev Mr Patton,[16]

Rev. & Dear Sir:

The friends of *Compensated Emancipation* propose to hold a Nat. Convention next month. The *Call* has already been signed by hundreds of influential men of all parties & professions, from Maine to Nebraska—including 100 from *Delaware* alone. The Venerable Dr *Nott*, Dr Hawes, Dr Bacon, Pres Mark Hopkins, & other distinguished Divines have given their names and adhesions. If you can approve of this pacific & generous arrangement to extinguish slavery will you not kindly sign the enclosed copy of the *Call* and forward it to me by *return of post*, if convenient, as the time is short.

I hope we may see you at the Convention, to speak a word in favor of its great object.

With Sincere Respect
Yours Truly
Elihu Burritt

MSS. COLLECTIONS
Library of Congress

---

[15] Liberal periodical sponsored by the Quaker philanthropist, Joseph Sturge.

[16] William Patton (1798-1879), antislavery clergyman and author.

New Britain, Conn., July 22, 1857

Gerrit Smith Esq.

My Dear Friend,

The work goes bravely on. I wish you could see the volume of letters & hundreds of names received to the *Call*.[17] ONE HUNDRED FROM DELAWARE ALONE! Is not that Capital? And some of the names are worthy to stand with the *first* attached to the *Call*—which was your *own*. We have Dr *Nott*,[18] Bacon,[19] Hawes, [20] Bethune,[21] Mark Hopkins,[22] Prof Upham [23] etc. I think Prof Silliman [24] will sign & attend the convention. I am still writing especially hoping to get some from Virginia, Maryland, Missouri etc.

Still think we must publish the *Call* in the newspapers by the Ist. of August. That *day* will be appropriate for the first appearance of the letters of invitation to meet in Cleveland to inaugurate a movement for Compensated Emancipation. Now my Dear friend will you not generously buckle on your best energies for the demonstration? How much will depend upon your presence. All my other old friends & comrades have abandoned me and rejected all participation in this undertaking. You know how much I have worked in the cause; but my efforts will break down without your aid—you will be at the Convention in good

---

[17] The "call" for a national convention for promoting the compensated emancipation project.

[18] Eliphalet Nott (1773-1866), Presbyterian clergyman and president of Union College.

[19] Leonard Bacon (1802-1881), Congregational clergyman, professor at Yale Divinity School and leader in the antislavery cause.

[20] Joel Hawes (1789-1867), author and Congregational minister at Hartford, Conn.

[21] George Washington Bethune (1805-1862), Dutch Reformed clergyman, staunch Democrat and opponent of slavery

[22] Mark Hopkins (1802-1887), president of Williams College.

[23] Thomas C Upham (1799-1872), distinguished authority on metaphysics, professor at Bowdoin College and leader in many reform causes.

[24] Benjamin Silliman (1779-1864), distinguished scientist and professor of natural philosophy at Yale College.

season? We may rely on that? And you will assist at its organization?

Who will we have for President? What say you to the venerable *Dr Nott!* His heart is in the cause. Would not his age, position, reputation for Prudence & Wisdom give the movement that character which we would impress upon it at the beginning? It strikes me that the President should be from New York State. Don't let us give the *New England Couleur* prominence at the outset.

Next; would it not be well to have say 3 or 6 Resolutions prepared before hand, developing any point or principle we wish to bring before the people; also have speakers prepared to develop each a point? In this case would it be safe & proper to ask certain persons to speak on this & that point immediately; that they may have time to elaborate some arguments with more care than they could do extemporaneously? Will you suggest a few points which I can send around to different parties? It seems to me we must have a small volume published of the speeches and proceedings in Convention, as we did in connection with the Peace Congresses in Europe.

Prof Silliman asks, if its intended that a National Emancipation Society shall be organized, and local associations established, as one of the results of the Convention.

Do drop me a line soon.

Ever Faithfully Yours,
Elihu Burritt

GERRIT SMITH MILLER COLLECTION
Syracuse University

[MS. JOURNALS]

[Taunton, Mass.] April 4 [1857]

Called upon ex-Gov. Morton [25] and had a long talk with him. Think he will sign the call for a Convention. Went on

[25] Marcus Morton (1784-1864), Democratic governor of Massachusetts 1839-1841 and life-long opponent of slavery.

to New Bedford, and was met at the station by Ezra Kelly, who took me to his house, and afterward called with me upon many of the citizens. Had an excellent and very influential audience in the evening. Most of the leading men were present, including the Friends. Among others, W. L. *Garrison* was before me taking notes, for the purpose [of] "pitching into me" the next day; as he had come on to speak on the Sabbath.[26] All listened with great attention: and three fourths voted for the plan.

[Boston] Wednesday, April. 8 [1857]

This was a great day for me—one long to be remembered. Friends Walker and Blanchard went with me to the State House at 7. It soon began to fill rapidly; and when I arose to speak, hardly a seat remained unoccupied. Mr Walker presided and introduced me with a few remarks. Most of the audience were men and members of the Legislature. I spoke with a good deal of animation and was listened to with close attention. Mr Walker took a vote on the appropriation of the Public Lands to the extinction of Slavery, and the *Ayes!* were almost unanimous. Not a No was heard. This was a great meeting.

[New Britain] Thursday July 23. [1857]

A rainy day; which to me was very grateful, as it enabled me to do up considerable writing. Feel the pressure heavy upon me. How soon will the days appointed for the Convention arrive! [27] All the enterprizes which I have launched be-

---

[26] In view of the rapidly rising price of slaves, and the opposition of Southern leaders to anything which questioned the morality and wisdom of slavery, Garrison thought that Burritt's movement was "preposterous." *William Lloyd Garrison, 1805-1879. The Story of His Life, Told by His Children* (N. Y., 1889), Vol. III, p. 461.

[27] The Convention met at Cleveland, August 25-27, and was well attended by delegates from several states. The National Compensation Emancipation Society was established. Prof. Benjamin Silliman of Yale was appointed president, but later refused to accept the office. Headquarters, with Burritt in charge, were established in New York.

fore this have broken down. The League of Brotherhood is dead. I gave to it ten of the best years of my life; but it could not live, while I was absent from England. The Christian Citizen died because of my absence from America. The Ocean Penny Postage movement is suspended. The Free Labor undertaking has miscarried.

[New York] Tuesday Oct. 13 [1857]

Second day of my *Secretariat.* Wrote from 8 till 5, more hours than I have written for a year or two. Commenced an exposition of the objects of our Soc. to be sent around to enlighten people and secure members. Wrote a letter to Dr Hopkins, Post, J W. Tatum & E. Fairbanks,[28] our Vice Presidents. Have not yet heard from Dr Hopkins and know not whether he will accept the post of Vice President. If he does, we shall regard him as our *Premier* and President, now that Prof Silliman has declined so peremptorily. A day of deepening gloom. Thirteen Banks have closed today, and a universal suspension must follow. I fear our little fund is gone.

Wednesday Oct 14 [1857]

. . . Have only about $1 left of what I borrowed of F. Burritt. Have put myself on short allowance of 25 cents a day for food. But can get more for this, than I have hitherto for 50 at the saloons. Intend to get a little office bed and sleep in my room, & prepare my own meals. Think I may thus get on for $2 a week. All the Banks of the City have suspended today.[29]

[New Britain] Friday Nov. 13 [1857]

Wrote again till dinner; and worked on the hill till night. Have now got in most of my little crop of corn & beans; have two more patches of turnips to gather. So shall have nearly fodder enough to carry the cattle & calves through the

[28] Erastus Fairbanks (1792-1864), inventor of the improved platform scale and twice governor of Vermont, 1852-1854 and during the Civil War.
[29] This was the beginning of the panic of 1857.

winter. Have received back the articles I wrote for the Nashville *Banner*, Dover *Reporter* & Baltimore *American*. Have not heard from those to Louisville *Journal*, Mo. *Republic*, & Frankfort *Yeoman*. The editors in the Slave States are determined to admit no discussion on the subject of *Emancipation*. So I must depend upon private letters.

Friday, Jan. 1, *1858*

. . . . Went on to Canandaigua where I had a small but very respectable audience in the evening. They gave me a good hearing, and I spoke with a good deal of animation and energy. Full three fourths of the men present signed the petition to Congress, including the editors of all the papers of the town. This was encouraging; and shows how all parties sympathise with the movement. . . .

[Trenton][30] Thursday Jan. 29 [1858]

This was a great day for me, which buoyed me up with new courage & hope. The speakers of the House of Reps & President of the Senate read my note to them, inviting the members of both bodies to attend my Lecture. To my great encouragement, the Governor and nearly two-thirds of the Members were present, with a goodly number of the citizens of Trenton. They gave me an excellent hearing to the end, and the impression seemed to be very favorable. The Gov. and others testified their approbation at the close. This was the most important audience I have addressed.

New Britain, Connecticut U.S.A.

May 26 1861

Rev Henry Richard

My Dear Friend.

I want to send you a few lines to thank you for your able, impressive and complete reply to friend Amasa Walk-

[30] The previous day Burritt had enjoyed a favorable reception at Princeton College, several professors and students signing the petition to Congress. A few days later at Lancaster, Pennsylvania, Thaddeus Stevens, member of Congress, introduced him at a lecture, after which two-thirds voted in favor of the plan of compensated emancipation.

er's letter.[31] I hope it will tend to arrest his honest mind from the insidious drifting that has carried nearly all our peace friends into the wake of this war. It has indeed been a *sifting* time here. I have been saddened and amazed at the spectacle. Men who we thought stood strong & firm upon the rock, have been washed away. I have almost trembled for dear Walker. His nature is warm and impulsive, and all his sympathies run out so exuberantly for a struggle for freedom versus Slavery. His son is an adjutant general in the army, and every influence works to wash him into the rushing current of popular sentiment. This is *entre nous seulement.*

He is my dearest friend on this side of the water. I hope your letter will recover him to his old footing. The great trouble with professed friends of peace here, is the habit of working up fictitious premises, then building an argument and a policy upon them. Mr. Beckwith [32] in the Advocate, has done a great deal to commit the Peace Society to this quicksand footing. He has assumed from the beginning that this terrible conflict, in which each party is arraying 500000 armed men against the other, is not *war,* but quelling a mob on the part of the Federal Government, that the Northern army of half a million is only a sherifs *posse* called out to put down an organisation of riotous individuals. I feel that this sophistry and position have shorn the locks of the Society of all the strength of principle; and I have been saddened to silence. I fear that 49 in a hundred of all the *Quakers* in America have drifted from their moorings in this storm of passion or indignation. This is truly a *trial hour.* All the ministers of the gospel, the religious press, all

[31] Merle Curti, *Peace or War · the American Struggle 1636-1936* (N. Y., 1936), pp. 50-51.

[32] The Rev. George C. Beckwith, secretary of the American Peace Society from 1837 to his death in 1873, had long seemed to Burritt to be compromising in his peace principles. See Curti, *The American Peace Crusade, 1815-1860, passim.*

classes of the community have been swept into the current. I have felt distressed at my inability to put forth a feather's weight of influence against the war spirit. In the first place no Northern journal would admit an article against the conflict. Indeed a religious paper in Philadelphia was supressed because it called it an *Unholy War*. The position taken by the Advocate of Peace completely nullifies that as an exponent of our fundamental principles, and there is no possibility of getting a hearing of a public audience for views adverse to the war.

Still I have ventured to lecture a few times on a plan of adjustment, involving a partial separation of the Southern & Northern States; but though I had a respectful hearing, the whole people go for a *vigorous prosecution* of *the war*, to the bitter end. I have gone as far as I could, without exposing myself to arrest in opposing the war; but I feel powerless and almost alone. Dear old Father *Blanchard* [33] of Boston, stands strong as a mountain of iron, and I hope there are a few scattered through the country who hold steadfastly to our principles. I am glad you view the Compensated Emancipation scheme as one which would have prevented the war, if adopted a few years ago. I am writing articles for the press tending to allay the fierce tide of indignation. I think our President will not sanction any measure of general confiscation to exasperate the South to a greater malignity of hatred, and thus perpetuate their animosity against us.—How I long again to see old England— to see the faces of old friends there once more in the flesh! How I should like to go out again with you to speak on peace in those towns we visited ten years ago! I live over those days; their remembrance grows more and more dear to me. If my life and health be spared, I intend to leave for England about the 1 st of October next, to spend the win-

---

[33] Joshua P. Blanchard was a Boston merchant who labored faithfully in the peace movement from 1834 until his death in 1868. See Curti, *Peace or War: the American Struggle 1636-1936*, pp. 59-60, pp. 76-77.

ter as a visit. I shall be very glad to get even a few lines
from you

Ever & faithfully Yours
Elihu Burritt

MS. COLLECTIONS
Friends House Library

New Britain, Conn.
Dec 13 1861

Mr E. W. Coggeshall,
    Dear Sir,
    My delay of a few days in answering your note has been
unavoidable. It may perhaps be possible that I shall lecture
in New York during the present winter, as I am anxious to
get a hearing for "A Plan of Adjustment and Reunion,"
which I have endeavored to develope. Should I have an opportunity to present this subject, I hope that I may have
your presence in the audience

Yours Truly
Elihu Burritt

BURRITT MSS.
Library of the Institute of New Britain

New Britain, Dec. 26, 1861

Hon. Chas. Sumner
My dear Sir
    It has been a long time since any communication has
passed between us, but I have always cherished the liveliest
interest in your position and progress as a leader through
the wilderness of sin, in which our nation is now well nigh
surrounded.
    You have always been kind and hospitable to my fan-
tasies, and now I want to commend to a moment's notice
"A Plan of Adjustment and Reunion", partially developed
in the enclosed.[34] Will you kindly run your eye over it,

---

[34] There is no accompanying document attached to the letter.

and give a little thought to the proposition, in its application to the double embroglio in which we are involved.

Yours ever truly,

Elihu Burritt

SUMNER MSS., *Letters Received*, Vol. LIV
Harvard College Library

New Britain, Jan. 1, 1862

Hon. Charles Sumner
My dear Sir

I beg you to excuse me for writing to you so soon again. You are chairman of the committee on Foreign Relations, and the friends of Peace are very hopeful that you will be instrumental of *great* good to the cause in this important position.

Now "*Honest Old Abe*" will adopt any suggestion of yours on international comity. Will you kindly ask him to reach his long arms across the ocean and drop a large burning coal right on the top of John Bull's head? It will melt down the proud pugnacity of his heart; and make him feel that there are some family affinities which his boisterous blustering cannot extinguish.[35] I mean that the President shall write a good honest letter to the Queen conveying to her the sentiment of condolation and sympathy that this nation feels for her in this hour of bereavement.[36] He can do it, and do it well.

Under these peculiar circumstances, nothing could be more magnanimous, more beautiful and touching than such a letter. She would prize it more than all the letters she will get from her European Sovereigns. Its effect would be most impressive on the English mind. But you need no one to suggest the propriety and value of such a communication. How I wish you would bring this about! You can do it by

[35] English feeling was at this time considerably aroused against the United States on account of the *Trent* affair.

[36] Albert, the Prince Consort, had recently died.

a bare suggestion: for the President would greatly enjoy the act.

Ever Truly Yours,
Elihu Burritt.

SUMNER MSS., *Letters Received*, Vol. LV
Harvard College Library

New Britain, Conn., Oct. 2, 1862.

Hon. S. P. Chase,[37]

Dear Sir,   Men who have attained to great eminence and power by their talents and virtues, must frequently revert with interest to the early stages of their upward career, and sometimes remember those who were associated with them, as it were, on an equal footing, in a common cause. I think you must often call to mind the old *Liberty Party,* and the struggle of that lone few against the powerful many, and remember some of the humble but earnest men who worked in the rank and file of that arduous campaign. Perhaps you will remember that I was one of that number, and labored in my small way to advance the cause we espoused. My first vote in a Presidential Election was given to *James G. Birney.*[38] Should this reach you at a moment when you may be recurring to those times, I will hope that you may be disposed, *"for auld lang syne,"* to give a moment to the consideration of *"A Plan of Adjustment and Reunion,"* which is partially developed in the enclosed paper written about a year ago. Although some of the premises of the argument have been modified in the interval, still I feel that the proposition, pure and simple, might be realized, and not only restore to us practically, the Old Union, in all its entirety and power, but also realise those larger and legitimate ambitions which we have long indulged as a nation.

[37] Salmon P. Chase (1808-1873), statesman, Secretary of the Treasury under Lincoln and Chief Justice during Reconstruction. For Chase's reply see J. W. Schuckers, *The Life and Public Services of Salmon P. Chase* (N. Y., 1874), p. 380.

[38] James G Birney (1792-1857), Southern antislavery leader and presidential candidate of the Liberty Party.

There is an impression abroad, that, before the first drop of blood stained the palm of the nation, you advocated, in the Cabinet, the principle and policy which Abraham adopted towards Lot, and preferred a peaceful separation of the Cotton States, to the terrible alternative which is now bleeding the country at its bluest veins. It is partly for this reason that I have ventured to address these lines to you. Perhaps at some future day, when you may have retired from public life, I may have the opportunity of thanking you in behalf of the friends of Peace, for the position you then took.

With great Respect & Esteem,
Yours Truly
Elihu Burritt

SALMON P. CHASE MSS.
Library of Congress

New Britain, Conn. Oct. 27, 1862

[To the Rev. Henry Richard,
  Secretary of the Peace Society, London]

My Dear Friend

Your kind & welcome letter has just arrived, and I hasten to write by return of post. If you will revert to my last letter, I think you will find that I fully intended to be in England by the 1 st of December—in the first week of that month ready to fulfil any engagements you might make for me. There are so many things to clean up here before leaving, so much to do and provide for, that I found myself much crowded when I wrote last. The days slip away, and my work diminishes slowly. Therefore, I am rather glad you have no positive engagements for me in the month of December; for I should like to spend a few weeks in London before going out on a lecture campaign. Now, then, if I am alive & well, I will leave on the 1 st of December, arriving probably in Liverpool about the 12 th. Will come up directly to London, perhaps stopping over night at Birmingham.

This will give me a few weeks with you, before going out to meet the engagements you may make for me. I do not recollect where Herbert Street is: if it were perfectly convenient & agreeable, I should be glad to get a cheap lodging somewhere near our old quarters about New Broad Street—just for *auld lang syne*, and to be near the office of the Peace Society. But this can all be arranged after my arrival perhaps.

If I should have elaborate writing to do, I should want a little secluded room by myself, were it no bigger than 6 by nine feet. Perhaps such a room with a grate in it might be found at your lodgings. It would be glorious & capital if we could be under the same roof, for I have such a world of things to say and ask.

Your most unexpected and generous offer to send me money for my passage, lifted a mountain load of anxiety from my mind; for I have lain awake nights think [ing] how I could clear up my floating debts here, and raise money enough to pay my passage even in the steerage. I do feel indeed grateful and joyful over this offer, for it will make the way clear before me. I think I told you before that I had to meet a large payment this autumn which I expected to get another years extension on, and this put me to great straits, so that providing for this payment, wiping out all my floating debts, raising money to pay my passage would have been a very heavy undertaking. But how will you be able to remit me such a sum? Who will advance it on such security as I can give? I hope you personally will not be put to any inconvenience on account of it. Whoever is so liberal and kind as to help me in this way will have my everlasting gratitude—You know, that in regard to my personal expenses, I am as close as a miser. I never incurred debts for personal comforts. For 20 years, my outlay for clothes, boots & shoes has not exceeded £5 per annum. Since the 1 st of January last it has not reached £2.— With regard to the state of public feeling in England towards the Northern States, I think I could go through the trials you speak of, without showing an unpleasant sensibility.

I know my position would be rather uncomfortable, and perhaps more so from the fact that I have from the beginning been opposed to this war not only on principle but on policy. Therefore, I could not elaborate or urge any arguments in its favor in England, because I condemn it here up to almost the prison door. Still if I could do anything to soften the unfriendly feeling of the English mind towards the North, I should be exceedingly glad. I am confident that my position could not be more embarrasing in England than it is here—for I am regarded here as almost a *secessionist*; and indeed, I only try to modify that impression by calling myself a *separationist*. The day grows darker and darker with us. The sacrifice in blood and treasure has been tremendous, and the end seems not a whit nearer than it did a year ago. The South has waged a terrible conflict for their independence—they have developed an energy, a willingness and capacity of endurance that have had few parallels in history. They are fighting under the most inflaming motives that can act upon a people— to secure their independence,—to save themselves from the humiliation of defeat and the fearful chastisement which they believe would follow their subjugation—and to save themselves from the crash and ruin of the slave system. I believe there is even a species of admiration in the North for this pluck, bravery, genius and persistance. I think, *entre nous*, that millions of the North covet the talent, dash and bravery of some of the Southern generals and that they would gladly give half a dozen of their own major generals for such a leader as old *"Stonewall"* A winter of discontent is rapidly coming on, and the people are fearing that the Federal army will soon go into winter quarters again, leaving the end postponed to some indefinite future. In the meantime, the unity of the North is being broken by the secession of a large portion of the Democratic party from the support of the Government. The policy of the Presidents Proclamation [of emancipation] is serving as a basis for that movement against the party in power. For myself I see no light in the working of that proclamation. If it goes into general effect, either the whites or the negroes of the South will have to evacuate that section, especially if the slaves should be armed and assist in the subjugation of their former masters. But President Lincoln is very cautious and conservative. He does not mean to incite the slaves to insurrection, and I doubt if he even consents to arm them against the South even as a *military necessity*. Of course, his proclamation will lie inoperative until the Southern States are pretty much all subjugated, for as fast as the federal armies march southward, the negroes will be withdrawn into the Gulf States.—Mr Gladstone's remarkable Speech will produce no little excitement both North & South.

No British Statesman is held here in higher estimation, and his weighty words will have all the more effect from being tempered with kindly sentiments toward the Northern people. But no Engish statesman can fully realise how the American heart clings to the idea and name of *Union*. All the previous histories hopes aspirations & ambitions of the Northern people cling to it as the sheet anchor of their political being. I heard a considerate, unexcitable Republican of the first standing among our citizens say a few days ago, that he would rather see slavery spread all over the Free States than to see the Union dissolved permanently. I have not a doubt that millions of the North would rather accept Jeff. Davis and his constitution, than consent to separation.—But we will talk over all this when we meet.—I do indeed deeply sympathise with you on the condition of your Hurbert. It is indeed a heavy dispensation for you to bear; but I hope you will all have the grace given you to bear it, and that he may rally again as he did before. Your other sons must be now much help to you. If I could only have had one of them to help me on my farm this year, I should have felt strong. As it is, I have not hired a single day's work of a man this season.— To conclude, I now fully intend and shall prepare to leave for England in the first week of December, so that you may make as definite arrangements as to *dates* from the 1st of January as you please. If you could remit me a draft for the £15 you generously propose to raise, so that I can get it by the 1st of December, it would be just in season. I will write again soon, and hope to hear from you once more before I leave.

Ever & Faithfully yours
Elihu Burritt

MS. COLLECTIONS
Friends House

35 Exchange,
Birmingham,
June 8 / 65

[To Thomas H. Dudley] [39]
Dear Sir

I do not think I could distribute any of the publications you refer to advantageously. As the war is over now, and the great work of reconstruction inaugurated, all good and patriotic men both North and South must feel it desirable and necessary to the restoration of the Union, to bridge chasms, heal wounds, and bleach the earth from blood, in a word, to let by-gones be by-gones as soon as possible. No human nor divine power can civilise war—especially civil war—and I am inclined to think the sooner the records of

---

[39] Thomas H. Dudley, United States Consul at Liverpool from 1861 to 1872, had recently asked consuls in England to distribute copies of the *Narrative of the Sufferings of Our Prisoners in the Hands of the Rebel Authorities,* a propaganda pamphlet prepared by the United States Sanitary Commission. Dudley to the Acting Secretary of State, Liverpool, May 12, 1865, in THOMAS H. DUDLEY COLLECTION, Henry E. Huntington Library.

atrocities on both sides of this long and terrible conflict are buried in oblivion, the sooner will a better future dawn upon our country.

Yours Truly
Elihu Burritt

THOMAS H. DUDLEY COLLECTION
Henry E. Huntington Library and Art Gallery

CHAPTER V

ASSISTED EMIGRATION AND ARBITRATION

IN 1863 Burritt returned to England, partly to promote better relations between the two countries, and partly to indulge his long-postponed dream of enjoying a leisurely walking trip from London to John O'Groats, the northernmost tip of Scotland. The book which he wrote[1] describing this experience abounds with picturesque and poetical descriptions of natural scenery and rural life.

In 1865 Burritt was made consular agent at Birmingham, a post which involved him in financial loss, and, as his letter to Hamilton Fish, Secretary of State, indicates, no end of troubles. He was able, however, to resume his work for "assisted emigration" to America. He had become interested in the emigrant during his first residence in England, and the League of Universal Brotherhood had incorporated aid to the emigrant in its platform. Aware of the hardships and exploitation to which the emigrant to America was subjected, Burritt hoped, through his plan of "assisted emigration," to rescue "the great transportation of peoples from the Old World to the New, from the heartless money-making

---

[1] *Walk from London to John O'Groats* (London, 1864). Burritt wrote a similar book describing another tour on foot, *Walks in the Black Country and Its Green Borderland* (London, 1866). This is particularly interesting on account of his observations on waste in coal mining, and by reason of his evaluations of trade and industry in this part of England. Seward, Secretary of State, expressed great satisfaction with the character and value of this book.

speculators." [2] Burritt now, as consular agent at Birmingham, wrote an introduction to George Washington's *Words to Intending English Emmigrants to America.* [3] In his introduction he gave expression to his resentment of the fact that promoters having special interests in certain regions had misrepresented them to credulous emigrants.

He then provided accurate and helpful information, particularly in regard to climate, health and economic opportunities, for the various regions of the United States. Burritt showed himself to be a pioneer in the field since known as human geography.

During his consulship in Birmingham (1865-1869) Burritt was also largely instrumental in forming the International Land and Labor Agency. The purpose of this organization was to find in advance work for emigrants, so that they would not need to drift about and lose time and money in seeking situations after their arrival. [4]

This wholesome project may have saved many immigrants from the clutches of agents who enticed the ignorant into signing contracts for wages which, in terms of American costs of living, were deceptive. In less than three months after the Agency began its work, more than a thousand farms, from Maine to California, were committed to it for sale to prospective emigrants, who could rest assured of fair dealing.

The last active efforts that Burritt made for world peace were more conservative in character than his earlier

[2] Burritt, MS. *Journal,* Nov. 14, 1846; *Christian Citizen,* Feb 13, May 1, 1847.

[3] Washington's letter was written to Sir John Sinclair in 1796.

[4] See *Herald of Peace,* May 1, 1879, p. 240, for Henry Richard's estimate of the achievements of this organization.

ones. His interest in the codification of the laws of nations, as a preliminary step toward a court of nations, was accentuated during the Civil War by the Anglo-American controversies over the *Trent,* the *Alabama* and neutral and belligerent rights generally.[5] In this campaign he did not work singlehanded: the distinguished American jurist, David Dudley Field, called attention to the desirability of codification of the laws of nations in an address delivered in 1867 before the British Social Science Association. Burritt also found in the Rev. James B. Miles, an officer of the American Peace Society, an invaluable coadjutor.

Shortly after his return to America in 1870, Burritt and Miles, marooned by reason of a storm in a hotel at New Bedford, drew up a call for a convention of American lawyers and jurists to form an internation code association. As a result of this initiative the Association for the Reform and Codification of the Laws of Nations was organized. Arrangements were made for sending Burritt and Miles to Europe to promote the project, but a railway accident prevented the learned blacksmith from making the voyage. From the platform in America, however, Burritt contributed to the success of the new organization,[6] and, from time to time spoke out in behalf of international sanity and world peace.

During his consulship Burritt did effective work for Anglo-American friendship, which had been seriously strained by reason of the conflict over the *Alabama Claims.*[7] Charles Sumner, to whom pacifists had long

---

[5] *Bond of Brotherhood,* new series, No. 157, Aug., 1863, pp. 120ff.

[6] James B. Miles, *Association for the Reform and Codification of the Laws of Nations. A Brief Sketch of its Formation* (Paris, 1875).

[7] "A New Way to Pay Old Debts" in *The Western and Eastern Questions of Europe* (Hartford, 1871).

looked for leadership, disappointed them by demand-
ing indirect or "consequential" as well as direct damages
from England for her negligence as a neutral during
the Civil War. Burritt did not hesitate to take to task
his old friend for what appeared to be an unreasonable
as well as a chauvinistic position. He also appealed to
both peoples to settle the controversy by resort to arbitration and naturally regarded the Geneva award as a
great victory for that principle. To consolidate this gain
for peace he spoke at many public gatherings in England, and addressed thirty meetings in America, in each
case pointing out the effectiveness of arbitration as a
method of settling international disputes. An old English friend, Henry Richard, observed that his voice was
weak and "a little vibrating," that he was frequently
interrupted by fatigue, and that his whole demeanor
bore evidence of excessive labor. But his spirit, Richard
continued, was unbroken, and he produced on his audiences "an extraordinary effect." [8]

During the later years of his life Burritt followed
European politics with keen interest. He had seen
through the humanitarian pretexts by which England
and France had tried to justify their imperialistic course
in the Crimean War, and had condemned the whole venture.[9] When Napoleon III issued his call for an international disarmament conference Burritt was disappointed that England turned down his invitation; he
could see, however, that there were reasons for England's
suspicions of the motives of the French emperor in calling the congress.[10] Against imperialism of every sort

[8] *Meeting à Londres, 17 Mai, 1870, Bibliothèque de la Paix* (Paris, 1871),
p. 7.
[9] *Bond of Brotherhood*, new series, Dec., 1856; June, 1856.
[10] *Bond of Brotherhood*, new series, no. 161, Dec., 1863, p. 185.

the learned blacksmith fought unwearying battles. His admiration of England did not keep him from excoriating her for her treatment of her subject peoples in India. "What a reign of Satanic devastation we have in India," he declared. "The inhuman burnings and butcherings perpetrated there by a people that arrogates to itself the first rank in Christian profession, are too terrible for reading." [11] Likewise British and French imperialistic wars for the opium trade in China met with the stern disapproval of the American friend of peace.

But his health was too broken to permit him to continue his arduous labors in behalf of humanitarianism. The man who had on countless occasions complained in his *Journal* of a hacking and persistent cough, of a feverish condition, and of excessive fatigue was now at best able to spend a few hours each day cultivating the soil of the little farm that he had purchased in New Britain.

Perhaps he was encouraged to resume his study of languages by reason of the fact that in 1872 he was given an honorary Master of Arts degree by Yale University. Two years later he published a *Sanskrit Handbook*, probably the first book in that language written by an American. He prepared, moreover, simplified grammars and reading exercises in Hindustani, Persian, Turkish, Arabic and Hebrew. And he taught Sanskrit to a group of high school girls at the moment when the first colleges for women had not yet demonstrated the capacity of that sex for higher learning.

In these last years, moreover, Burritt's mind turned increasingly toward the problem of religion. All his life he had been a deeply religious man and had opposed narrow sectarianism and whatever stood in the way of truly

---

[11] *Bond of Brotherhood*, new series, no. 96, July, 1858, p. 184.

spiritual values. On his return to America in 1870 he wrote, in an assumed style and anonymously, a book entitled *A Voice from the Back Pews*. The "back pew man," was, of course, Elihu Burritt himself. He describes the agony wrought to his boy's mind by the stern and horrible sermons of the Calvinist preacher to whom he listened, and then proceeds to trace the history of his spiritual emancipation. This book, which is that of a mystic, is charged with a belief in the continuity of divine inspiration in the daily walks and the little things of life. From his workshop there came also *Prayers and Devotional Meditations, collated from the Psalms of David* (New York, 1869) and *Children of the Bible* (New York, 1873). And bent on practicing as well as preaching, he built, with his own hands and at his own expense, a little chapel for those living in the outlying districts of New Britain. Here "union" meetings were held which did much to break down the spirit of sectarianism.

This is not the occasion to speak in further detail of the thirty books and of the periodicals for which Burritt's hand and mind were responsible. Nor is it the place to comment on his forward-looking views on criminology and science. But a final word must be said of his childlike and beautiful personality, which made him beloved and welcome in a larger number of households than was any American of his time. "His singleness of devotion . . . fills me with reverence," Charles Sumner wrote. "Perhaps with more knowledge of the practical affairs of government he would necessarily lose something of that hope which is to him an unfailing succor." [12] Indeed, his courage and his faith, as well as his farseeing

[12] Edward L. Pierce, *Memoir and Letters of Charles Sumner*, Vol III (Boston, 1894), p. 74.

vision entitle him to respect. And his militant action in behalf of many unpopular social causes, radical in their day, makes a splendid chapter in the history of nineteenth-century humanitarianism.

15 New Broad Street, London, March 30 '49

S. D. Hastings.[13]

My Dear Friend,

Although you and I are separated by a broad expanse of sea and land, I remember you as one of the true friends of other days. In the midst of arduous engagements, I write you from this our Mother Land in which I am sojourning, desiring to send you some token of my kindly remembrance, also to ask your advice upon a question in which I feel a deep and increasing interest. I am convinced more than ever that our great country must supply homes to thousands or perhaps millions that are struggling for subsistence in Great Britain. I love America with a new affection from this circumstance, that it is to become an asylum and home to thousands of the toiling population of this and other European countries. And I feel anxious that the transplantation of these families from the Old World should create new ties of brotherhood between the two continents; that it should be conducted in a spirit of philanthropy and be blessed to all parties. I have long felt that it might be associated with the League of Brotherhood, as one of the departments of its labours. Great attention is now excited in England to the subject of emigration to the U. States, as well as to other parts of the world. Information is asked from all quarters about the proper localities, and the proper means and ways to reach them. I have many letters lying on my table asking this information. I have, therefore, thought to devote a column of the Citizen Weekly to this subject, and to invite our Western friends to send us accounts of their own localities, and the nearest or cheapest way to them. This information I would reprint in England, and send to those who inquire. Now I want to look to you to lead off in this matter. I know you would not be

---

[13] Hastings had moved to Wisconsin in 1846, and was a member of its first state legislature in 1848.

influenced by any pecuniary considerations, and therefore your statements might be relied on fully. I want to have you write an account of those lands which are for sale immediately *around you*, or in any part of Wisconsin, with which you are personally acquainted,—stating their *extent, locality, quality, price,* and the *nearest way to them* from New York or Boston; the *cheapest line of conveyance,* the *implements,* and other articles of use which the emigrant would do well to bring with him; the society which he would be a member of, the school and religious instruction which he could impart to his children, and answers to such other questions which you would like to ask were you an Englishman on the eve of emigrating to the United States, and not knowing where to go, what locality, or society to settle in, or how to reach it. To begin, suppose you should write a letter to *me* to be published in the Citizen, describing the *land* which might *be bought in your immediate neighborhood,* the price &c. Government land or that which has been partially cultivated. I suppose that 1000 acres at least might be bought near you from $1.25 to $5 per acre. This might be cut up into *6 farms,* as large as the emigrants from England would desire. Even this would do for an *experiment.*

We would send a circle of six families, or heads of families, who should pay for it and settle upon it. We should hope to send you a little community which would make you a good neighborhood, good citizens, well instructed in English agriculture, who should become perhaps *model farmers* for your country. Most of them would be *"brother Leaguers",* most industrious men. As such we should be glad to introduce them to you, hoping that you would receive them as brethren. Many of these will have a little capital, perhaps sufficient to buy a farm which is already under cultivation, with comfortable buildings upon it. And I suppose there must be a good many single farms of this kind for sale. If in addition to the other information which

I have asked, you would send to me copies of Wisconsin Newspapers containing *advertisements of such farms*, I could find *purchasers* here for them. But I hope you will be able to send to the Citizen without much delay, an account of the lands, cultivated or otherwise, in your neighborhood, town or county, which might be taken up and settled by little communities of English farmers. So permit me to look in the Citizen for such a letter from you, at your earliest convenience.

I am anxious that the transplantation of such a little community should be tried in your neighborhood, and upon your advice. I know your heart will sympathise with a movement of this kind, conducted on philanthropic principles & in a brotherly spirit. I would see that those who formed a part of the circle should be moral, respectable & industrious men, with a little capital, and who would be an aquisition of some value to your society.

Now that a new postal arrangement is effected between England & the U. S. A. I hope you will not only write the letter to the Citizen which I have solicited, but that you will write to me also direct to London. I hope you have seen accounts of my movements here, and of the great progress the peace cause has made during the last few years. Mr Drew will forward this letter to you, as I do not know exactly your location.

Fraternally & ever yours

Elihu Burritt

OBERLIN COLLEGE MSS.

Birmingham, March 28, 1867

Hon. Gerrit Smith.

My Dear Friend,

I was exceedingly gladdened to see your handwriting once more and to receive such a good kind letter from you. So many eventful years have passed since we last wrote to each other, but it seems as we had waked up in a new if not a better world in exchanging letters now.

—In the first place, then, I must thank you most heartily for your kind and generous words of sympathy called forth by the great loss we have sustained in the death of dear Edmund Fry.[14] I am glad and almost surprised that you have been able to find time to look into the *Bond*, as I send it to you chiefly that you may see by the handwriting on the cover that you live in my heart's remembrance. It is, indeed, a great and irreparable loss, which makes me feel lonely in the world. We were more than ordinary brothers by mere *blood*. Your words of sympathy to the widow and fatherless children are very precious to them. I am sure you will not regret their appearance in the April Bond. I thank you most cordially for the $10 you sent to be appropriated as I thought best. Now I thought, inasmuch as you had expressed such esteem of Mr Fry's character that it would be a pleasant tribute to his memory, which his friends here would value highly, if your gift should be added to the list of contributions for erecting a monument over his grave.

We would give his monument an *international* character, showing that he was appreciated and esteemed in America. I think you will approve of this idea and not think I have misappropriated your gift in putting it on the list of contributions to the Monument Fund as you will notice in the April Bond.—I am now giving more time & thought to the Bond than ever before. I could not bear the thought of letting it die with Mr. Fry; as it is the only visible tangible tie that connects me with causes for which I have labored so many years, and with hundreds with whom I have been associated in this country. So I have not only resumed the entire editorship of it but am filling it entirely with my own thoughts, hoping to raise its literary standard a little which had been a little lowered by inferior communications admitted into it from second rate writers.

[14] Edmund Fry was Burritt's chief English collaborator in the work of the League of Universal Brotherhood.

You will see the face of another Martyr-hero, who like Franklin, has laid down his life on the altar of Service. I have made a notice which I hope you will read and approve, though very brief and giving but little of his personal history. You will notice perhaps that I am bringing out a series of articles as the *Rise and Progress of "We"!* which will probably go through all the nos. for the present year. There I am talking to the children in the character of "Old Burchell," [15] on subjects which may interest you.

I have been in England this time a little over four years, and have travelled and written much in that space. For the first time in my life I have sat down to write whole books on continuous subjects. The only book I ever produced before was made up of selections from articles written for the *"Christian Citizen"* etc. I have walked from London to John O'Groats, and from London to Land's End and back, and made two great books on that enterprise each of 450 pages.

This last year I wrote *"The Mission of Great Sufferings,"* 250 pages, the best thing I ever did. The Bond contains extracts from these three books, some of which you may have noticed. I hope the books themselves may be published in America, so that you may see them. I would send them to you if there were a book postage, but the postage between these two great countries is still on a heathenish basis, niggardly and unworthy of civilization.

I am pleasantly situated here—the business is simple, merely commercial, and I am able to put forth some thoughts beyond the duties it invokes, while the income makes me easy and comfortable. I have two nieces from America residing with me which makes my little quiet home very enjoyable.

Faithfully & Ever Yours
Elihu Burritt

[15] These "talks" were published as *Old Burchell's Pocket* (London, 1866).

P. S. I have longed to write you my thoughts on the events that have shaken our country like an earthquake, and on the spirit which those events have called forth North & South. But I could not do it without writing a pamphlet which my present position would render it improper for me to do.

You are the only man in America to whom I would venture to express my mind freely & fully on these important subjects, not that you would agree with me in my views but that you would treat them hospitably, and not turn them out of doors because they did not coincide with the views of the great majority. But I think to this extent you would agree with me:

1. That you cannot hang a man and make a coffin for him out of his cradle.
2. That it takes a great deal of oil to put out a small fire; as has been proved in Poland, Hungary and Ireland.
3. That you cannot contrite and convert the rebellious spirit in a man by whipping his naked body with nettles.
4. That our constitution would as soon allow us to impose an absolute monarchy as the rule of a minority upon the people of any state inside or outside the Union.
5. That there is a *Sweets-of-Power* Party, as well as a "Bread-and Butter Party"—a very old Party in the history of the world which has always been punished by its own demoralisation for its revelling in the luxuries of oppression.

Here are five points or principles that I could write a small volume upon, which, perhaps, a few—a very few and unpopular men in America might read with the Sympathy of their conviction. But then it might do no good. . . .

E. B.

GERRIT SMITH MILLER COLLECTION
Syracuse University

Birmingham, Dec. 4 1868

To the Hon.

    W. H. Seward,

        Secretary of State,

           Washington.

Sir:

I am constrained, by new and pressing considerations, to address to you, for the first time, a direct communication on the subject of my position as Consular Agent of the United States at Birmingham. Mr Z. Eastman, U. S. Consul at Bristol, to whose Consulate this Agency belongs, has recently returned from the United States, and informs me that, when in Washington, he submitted to you a communication which I had addressed to him, and in which I stated some facts and considerations bearing upon the business and inevitable expenses of this Consular Agency. I learned with regret that these facts and considerations were not regarded as sufficient to modify the application of the strict letter of the recent Act of Congress to my case or the case of any one filling my position here. I, therefore, beg most respectfully to present for your favorable consideration a few additional statements, in the hope that they may avail to except my case from the rigid application of the Congressional Act to which I have referred.

In the first place, then, I am firmly persuaded that Congress, in the late Act limiting the compensation of Consuls and Consular Agents, did not intend to reduce such a Consulate as that of Birmingham to $1500 or $2000 a year for its expenses and for the compensation of the Consular Agent.

For this Consulate, both for the amount of business it transacts, and for the inevitable expense of transacting it, must be the very next in England after London, Liverpool, and Manchester, or the fourth in importance. It embraces not only the whole of the Black Country, but large manufacturing towns, such as Coventry and Redditch, beyond it. The value of the exports from the district certified here in 1866 amounted to a million pounds sterling. The Printing, Postage, Seals, Envelopes, Tape, Wax and transportation of parcels for that year cost £60.16.8. I paid my clerk £120.4 for his services during the year;—about £20 of this was for extra work, the business being so large that he had frequently to work until midnight to accomplish it. The rent of the office, rates and taxes, coal, gas, &c. brought up the expenditures of the consulate to full £250 for the year. Then there are other expenses inseperably connected with the Consulate. Almost every day some poor, distressed American sailor, or other needy American, importunes me piteously for help in food, or fare to Liverpool, or other port. They come in the most miserable condition, and feel that they have a claim on the U. S. Consulate for relief. I have not been able to refuse their pathetic appeals, and have been constrained not only to give them aid, but have subscribed £4.4 to the General Hospital here, in order to be able to give an indoor ticket to some poor sick American sailor. Although I have given but small sums to these suffering applicants, yet they have been so frequent and numerous, that I have not been able to pay out less than £20 a year for their relief since I have been in this office.

Then I am expected to subscribe, as Consul, to many local charities, and to be present at public dinners and occasions in honor of the incoming and outgoing Mayors; all of which involve expense, so that I can truly say, that my official expenses for the Consulate for 1866 cannot have been less than £300, without counting in a shilling for my own private or personal expenses. Thus, if the recent Act of Congress were so interpreted and applied as to reduce the whole allowance for the support of the Birmingham Consulate to Fifteen Hundred Dollars a year, I should not have had the value of a single meal of victuals for my services in 1866.—And if the said Act shall be so applied as to reduce

this Consulate to the allowance of *Two thousand Dollars* a
year, including all the expenses, and if the Department en-
forces upon me, direct or through Mr. Eastman, a reimbursement of all over that sum that I have received and
used as my compensation since the passing of the Act, then
such a reimbursement will sweep away not only all my as-
sets in England, but also my little farm of 40 acres in my
native town in Connecticut. To make this reimbursement, I
should have to sell at a reduced rate the copyrights of all my
books published in England before I took the Consulate;
and I should also be obliged to sell all my furniture, and all
the books of my small library, and also my small homestead
in America.

And, what would aggravate my mortification and distress,
this confiscation or forced sale would make me appear, both
here and at home, as a dishonest defaulter to the Government I had tried to serve faithfully and well.

My health has now become so impaired that I cannot look
to any new employment; and if I have to give back all that
I thought I had earned and saved during the last two or
three years, it will be a bitter grief to my last days. I feel
that I have tried to discharge the duties of this Consulate
faithfully. Indeed, I have essayed to do what few Consuls
ever attempt. I have endeavored to make the State Department and the American public more thoroughly and definitely acquainted with the productive capacities and mechanical industries embraced in the whole Black Country and
other sections included in the Birmingham Consulate. For
that purpose, I visited various towns and centres of Manufacture in the district, and described at length the processes
adopted, in detail and result; thinking that such descriptions might be useful to the Department and to the Manufacturers in the United States. These notes and Observations filled a large volume, and occupied all the leisure time
I could save from official duties through the whole year
1867. The Department has already received a copy of the

said work, entitled, "*Walks in the Black Country,*" and can easily understand the labour it cost, and appreciate the purpose and thought of the book. Of course, while visiting these various towns and Manufacturing Establishments, and writing out my observations for the volume, I was obliged to employ a responsible and intelligent clerk, of a high grade of capacity, to perform the routine work of the office, while I was thus employed. All these undertakings also increased my expenses; but I was anxious to convince the Department that I was doing my best to fill the Consulate faithfully and acceptably.

In view of these facts and considerations, I hope it may be within the discretion and power of the Department to put this very important Consulate on a footing somewhat nearer to that of other large towns in England. Without detaching it from Bristol, or making it an independent Consulate, I have thought the Department might be willing to allow *Twenty-five Hundred Dollars* a year for the whole expenses of the Birmingham Consulate, including the compensation of the Agent here;—he remitting through the head consul at Bristol, to the Department all the money received for fees above that amount.

This would make a difference between this and the Bristol Consulate of about $1000 in favor of the latter, as the Congressional Act allows the Consul there $2500 a year over and above the expense of office rent and clerk hire &c. As the annual expense of carrying on this Consulate must always be greater than that of Bristol, as probably two thirds of the total income and business of the whole district included in the Bristol Consulate come from Birmingham, I hope the Department will regard the allowance I have asked reasonable, equitable and necessary.

As this is the first communication that I have ever addressed directly to the Department, and as all my earnings and savings for nearly three years must be swept away, if the Congressional Act is to be rigidly applied to this Consulate, I hope that you will excuse the length and earnestness of this statement and application.

Awaiting an early and favorable reply,

> I have the Honor
> To remain
> Your Obed^{rt} Servant
> Elihu Burritt
> U. S. Consular Agent

Despatches, Bristol, Vol. II Birmingham
Department of State   England

Birmingham, Feb. 3, 1869

My dear Mr Sumner,

Although I have not written to you for several years, I have watched your course with as much lively interest, hope and faith, as if I saw you every week. These last 10 years have been full of mighty events of which you may well say "magna pars fui". For myself, I feel half stunned by these events, so that I cannot make them real and tangible verities to my mind.

But my especial object in writing now is, to beg you to remember that you were at the beginning the champion of Ocean Penny Postage in the U. S. Congress. It seems to be coming up again, and I hope this time it will become a *fait accompli.*

Let me beg you to add this great and beneficent reform to your other laurels. Since I used to talk with you on the subject in Washington, full 2 millions of emigrants from Europe have poured into the U. S. But you need to be reminded of no facts or arguments in favor of this boon to millions. For myself, I do not care to be mentioned or remembered in connection with the reform, but am very anxious to see it realised, and shall feel myself amply repaid for all my labour in the cause in the good it will bring to the poor on both sides of the Atlantic. There is a good deal of interest stirring up in England in its behalf, and everything seems ripe and ready for the reform. I am confident your influence will carry it through Congress; and that no one could see its benefits more clearly than yourself.

During this sojourn in England I have performed a good deal of literary labor; having written 3 large volumes on "Walks" in various directions,[16] besides two or three other books.[17] Feeling that I should not be able to address public meetings any more, I am making up my lectures and speeches into a volume, & hope to send you a copy of them when they leave the press.

I have been at this post as consular Agent nearly four years, and have found the duties quite pleasant. And now I want to thank you most gratefully for the kind interest you have manifested in my welfare, when I was under the impression that I was utterly ruined. I have seen a copy of a note which you addressed to Richard Parsons, Esq., on the subject, and I was much affected by your generous sympathy for me.

I confounded two acts of Congress with each other and got the idea that the act cutting down my allowance to $1500 a year ran back to July *1866*, whereas it only goes back to April *1868*, or only 3 quarters of the year just past. Although this allowance gives me only 2 thirds the amount it costs me to live very economically, still I feel grateful and even *rich* compared with the fear and consternation I experienced when I thought I was to be obliged to give back to the Department nearly all I had earned for 3 years. I think I can have $500 or $600 a year of the $1500 for my own personal support, and I get something from my books besides. So now I feel quite easy, relieved from the fears I

[16] *Walk from London to John O'Groats* (London, 1864); *Walk from London to Land's End and Back* (London, 1865); *Walks in the Black Country* (London, 1866).

[17] *Old Burchell's Pocket* (London, 1866); *The Mission of Great Sufferings* (London, 1867); *Jacob and Joseph* (London, 1868).

felt when I wrote my long letter to Mr. Seward on the subject. And now thanking you most heartily for all your kind & generous feeling toward me,

I am ever yours faithfully

Elihu Burritt

SUMNER MSS., *Letters Received*, Vol. LXXXIX
Harvard College Library

Birmingham, Feb. 26 /69

My dear Mr Sumner,

I beg you on the strength of long acquaintance and sympathy on great subjects to excuse my writing you again so soon. But the matter affects my interests very deeply. I have just heard that this consular agency has been set off from the Bristol District and erected into an *independent* consulate by itself, like that of Manchester, Liverpool, etc. Now if some one more deserving of the office has not been appointed already, I should like to be considered a candidate for it. I feel that I have given full satisfaction to the people of Birmingham and the Black Country included in this Consulate, and that they would be pleased to have me remain here as consul. I have become, to a certain extent, the historian of the town and district, and they esteem my "Walks in the Black Country" as the fullest and most popular history and description that has ever appeared. During my present sojourn in England I have performed a good deal of literary work and acquired some additional literary reputation, a quality which, perhaps, it would not be undesirable to associate with American officials abroad. I feel that I could fill the post acceptably to the State Department at Washington. I know I am not a political man, and have rendered no political service to the present Administration that would entitle me to the post by that claim on which office-seekers generally base their expectations. Still, perhaps the new regime will not attach so much importance to this claim as other administrations have done, and will give a few posts at least to those whose only merit is the ability and will to fill them faithfully.

As you are the only one to whom I can write with any hope of effect, I venture to ask you to say a good word for me in the right quarters, if you can do it consistently and properly.

I send you herewith a copy of my *Walks in the Black Country* and hope you will find leisure to glance at some of its sketches of character & scenery. The large edition is exhausted, or I would send you a copy of it, which is a pretty large book.

I hope you will read what John Bright said of *Ocean Penny Postage* in his speech before the House of Commons a day or two ago. Ever & truly,

I am yours

Elihu Burritt

SUMNER MSS., *Letters Received*, Vol. XC
Harvard College Library

Birmingham, Aug. 4 1869.

To Hon.

Hamilton Fish,

Secretary of State.

Sir:—I am constrained to address one more communication to the Department of State in regard to the peculiar position in which I have been situated during the past year as Consular Agent for Birmingham. I will not repeat the statements and arguments which I have already submitted to the Department. These have already been taken into consideration and acted upon liberally and promptly in behalf of my successor.

The District embraced in the Birmingham Consulate exports to the United States to the amount of nearly $5,000,-000 a year. Its business makes it probably the fourth Consulate in England in amount and in the cost of Consular Service upon it. Somewhat over a year ago an Act of Congress reduced my allowance for doing all this business to $1500 a year including expenses. Now I was obliged to have a convenient and respectable office in the centre of the town, and a first-rate clerk to perform the work of the consulate. The office, rent, taxes, gas, coal &c and the clerk hire cost me $1000 a year, leaving me only $500 a year for my personal services and support, which is less than a good Irish hod-carrier in America gets for his labor, and is not half what it has cost me to live in a frugal and decent way as Consular Agent. I am now in danger of having more than $100 a year deducted from this small pittance by the Act referred to. In each quarterly account which I have returned to Mr Z. Eastman, the U. S. Consul at Bristol, to which consulate the Birmingham Agency belonged, I credited to myself about $30 for printed or blank forms & Certificates, postage stamps, parcels delivery, seals, tape, consular envelopes &c &c. Mr Eastman has admitted these items of credit to me subject to the sanction of the Department only; and this is my reason for addressing this communication to you, to ask your interpretation of the law in my case.

The point I raise is this: That the items I have mentioned do not belong, under the law, to *expense* account, but to *capital* or *stock* account. I put it in this way: Suppose I engage to make hoes or axes for the Government, and to furnish shop, tools and labor, for $1,500 a year.

These are the expenses that devolve upon me clearly under the contract. But can the Government, under the term of *expenses*, compel me to furnish coal and iron, and pay for the transportation of the hoes to Washington? Is it not as clear as day that the more hoes I make the poorer I am, or the less I receive for my labor?

This is my point, and I think you will admit that it is the position of my case. The items I have charged the Department through Mr Eastman are the coal and iron and the transportation of the hoes I have supplied. I therefore claim and expect that the Department will admit my charge for these items, or allow Mr Eastman to credit them to me in my quarterly settlements with him. They amount to between £5 and £6 per quarter for the past year.

Hoping to receive an early and favorable reply to this application,

I am Your Obedient Servant

Elihu Burritt

Late U. S. Consular Agent at Birmingham

Despatches, Bristol, Vol. II

Department of State

Birmingham, Oct. 11, 1869

[To the Rev. J. Williams.]

My dear Sir

I write for Mrs Holmes, my associate in our agency,[18] of which I am the founder and for which I am willing to assume the responsibility as to its spirit and working. We can supply any number of good servant girls out of Shropshire and other agricultural counties at the shortest notice. Indeed we have a dozen waiting for definite orders on applications from America. But we find them much poorer than we even expected as to means. Not one in fifty can raise six guineas to pay his passage. At first we thought they would each raise *half* the passage money, but on inquiry, we find it is almost impossible for any of them to do even this. So the only condition on which they can go out is this; that the family or party sending a positive, definite order for a servant girl must forward to the Agency the whole passage money, sea & inland, that is £6.6 for sea, the English inland, say [sh.] 7.9; then the U. S. inland fare whatever it may be. In addition to this our agency has to charge each servant 10 s for the expense of advertising & correspondence in obtaining the situation. We have just sent off

---

[18] The International Land and Labour Agency, the purpose of which was to aid prospective emigrants to America.

three girls to Hollidaysburg, Pa. and have had to pay the following bills:

outfit of berth, bed, plate,	7.6
fare to Liverpool	7.6
expense in Liverpool	2.6
fare to New York	6.6.0
expense in New York	3.0
fare from N. Y. to Hollidaysburg,	1.6.0
fee to agency	.10.
	£9.1.6

From this statement you may estimate what it will cost to forward English girls to Boston. As there would be no inland expenses on arriving there, the whole expense from the center of England to Boston would be about £7.12. This amount must be forwarded to our agency, directly from or for the family employing the servant, to be deducted out of her first wages, though it would greatly encourage her to spread the repayment over six months labor, so that she could feel that she was earning something for herself the first week of service. We think we could send a good trusty English girl who would do all kinds of work by the return steamer, as we shall always have several waiting to go at six day's notice. The party applying for a girl must say how much they will give her per week & what service they expect.

Yours truly
Elihu Burritt

P. S. In case a professional cook, or a girl of some special service being required, some delay would be involved, as such a servant would have to give a month's notice to her present employers.

ELLEN W. WASHBURN PAPERS, Vol. XI
Massachusetts Historical Society

Birmingham, June 20 /70

Hon. E. B. Washburne [19]

  Sir

    I beg you to excuse my freedom in addressing this to you. But as your name embraces the whole of mine, I write with all the more confidence—I am collecting a memorial to Charles Dickens from the Press and Pulpit of different countries, and if you can approve of the work, I should be exceedingly obliged to you indeed, if you would send me any Illinois or other U. S. papers you may receive this week, containing notices of him, after you have read them through. I will send them back to you with many thanks, after I have copied out the notices. I ever hardly ask such a favor, but I should feel myself deeply beholden to you for it; if you would get some intelligent young man connected with your office to collect such French journals and periodicals as have noticed Dickens, and have them forwarded to me. I will gladly pay him well for his expense & labor.

  I think every country on the globe that publishes a newspaper will contribute to this memorial to Charles Dickens. Wishing you all success & happiness in your great position,

      I am yours truly

        Elihu Burritt

WASHBURNE MSS., Vol. XIX
Massachusetts Historical Society

    New Britain, Conn. July 17 /71.

Rev J-B. Miles [20]

  My Dear Sir,

    I thank you for your kind and interesting letter and am glad you have taken hold of the work as

---

[19] Elihu Benjamin Washburne (1816–1887) was born in Maine, practiced law in Galena, Illinois, was elected to Congress in 1852 and was minister to France at this time.

[20] James B. Miles, secretary of the American Peace Society from 1871 to 1876, was a clergyman.

secretary permanently located in Boston. I hope you will be able to effect all the improvement in the Advocate [21] and the cause itself that you wish. I am persuaded that if the Advocate could be brought promptly at the beginning of the month, it would be much gain to it. It now seems to lag behind other monthlies in this respect, giving the impression of being on lame legs. I am ready to do what I can to bring it up to time. You are welcome to keep and use my address. I think a celebration of the Treaty [22] very desirable; if my health and other circumstances will permit, I shall hope to be present. I hope, however, the demonstration will have no political aim or aspect, e u [?] to make capital for any political party.

Yours Very Truly
Elihu Burritt

MS. LETTERS FROM ELIHU BURRITT
American Peace Society

New Britain Ct. July 31 /71

Rev J. B. Miles
My Dear Sir,
        I was in New Haven a few days ago, and met there an old friend and neighbor, Rev Wm. Whittlesey. He is a native of New Britain whom I have known from boyhood. He expressed much interest in the peace cause, having read the publications of the Society for a long time. He thinks he could work for it advantageously not only in New Haven but in the State, by canvassing for subscribers and subscriptions in money. He could also get up public meetings on the subject, and stir up an interest in the cause. I encouraged him in this idea, and even promised I would attend a meeting in Hartford and New Haven with him to introduce him as your agent for the state if you should ap-

[21] *The Advocate of Peace* was the organ of the American Peace Society.
[22] The Treaty of Washington provided for the arbitration of certain Anglo-American disputes arising out of the Civil War.

point him as such. We have never had a live man in this state to represent the cause, and I think his heart is in it and would be perhaps the best man to be found. It would be especially gratifying to me to have a New Briton in the work. Now I hope you will see the way clear to appoint him an agent for Connecticut or at least for New Haven. If so, I hope you will do it at once, and send him authority to act, also, some copies of all your publications that he may sell or circulate them. I have 1000 copies still of my tract, "*Workingmen's Strike against War.*" They cost me $5. If you will credit me that sum, I will send the whole to him. Perhaps it might be well to allow him a certain *per centage* on all the money he collects for the Society. In this way he would pay himself for his time and labor and also collect something for your general operations.

Will you please consider this proposition and write to him if you accept it? Address Rev Wm Whittlesey, 107 Dwight Street, New Haven. He is ready to enter at once upon the work.

Yours Truly,
Elihu Burritt

MS. LETTERS FROM ELIHU BURRITT
American Peace Society

New Britain, Ct. Aug. 15 /71

Rev Mr Miles.

My Dear Sir,

I thank you for your kind and interesting letter. I am glad you were pleased with my suggestion of Mr Whittlesey as Agent for the State. I have just written him inviting him to go on with me to your proposed meeting, to make acquaintance with the friends of peace and get a little new inspiration. Will you please give a little notice of the date, so that we may prepare for the occasion? Have you fixed upon the *week* in Sept? I hope the demonstration will be in honor of the Treaty and be so conducted that no *political* sensitiveness will be aroused or affected: that it will not be suspected of making capital for any party. The ground is a little delicate at this time.

I am writing an Introduction to the Life of William Ladd. I hope the book will circulate widely. It is a beautiful life.

If Mrs Stowe would write a story with peace teaching, it would be of great value. I do not know if she feels that the cause is quite up to her level of literature. Still, it may be well to try her. I think she has left Hartford, but a letter addressed to her there would be forwarded.

As this Introduction will occupy me a week, perhaps you will not expect anything from my pen this month; but if you need it I will send you a page.

I am writing some little leaflets for Children of six years, in words of *one* syllable, to be called
"Dewdrops of the Law of Kindness
In Short Words
    For
Small Children."
I think you will like to copy them into your Advocate or Angel

Yours Truly,
Elihu Burritt

MS. LETTERS FROM ELIHU BURRITT
American Peace Society

New Britain, Ct. Sept 20 /71

Rev J. B. Miles
    My Dear Sir,
        I intend to start for Boston on Monday next, so as to be there all day on Tuesday. I hope Mr. Whittlesey of New Haven will go on with me. He is working nobly for the cause through the public press, perhaps writing more than anyone else in the country. I think he is a very valuable acquisition, and hope some arrangement will be

made to sustain him in the work—to compensate him fairly for his labor either out of the general receipts, or out of funds he may collect for the Society as its agent. I want to have you see and know him, and recognise him as one of the working corps. I have offered to see his railway fare to and from Boston paid, even if I do it out of my own pocket; for we could hardly ask him to make such a journey on his own charges, as he is virtually poor. All my old friends in Boston are gone, but I will go to a hotel on Tuesday night. If however someone will give Mr Whittlesey the hospitality of his house for the night, I shall be glad as well as he. I do not know if he has friends there; if he has, he will go to them. I have suggested that he should send a page of report of his labors during the month for the Oct. Advocate.

I am suffering with a terrible cold, but hope to be better before the meeting, and be able to speak 12 or 15 minutes. If Mr Sumner speaks, I suppose you will let his speech be the last. If convenient, I should like to speak early in the evening. I finished the Introduction to the Life of William Ladd [23] several weeks ago, & forwarded the MS. to Amasa Walker.

Yours Truly
Elihu Burritt

MS. LETTERS FROM ELIHU BURRITT
American Peace Society

New Britain, Ct. Oct. 9/71

Rev J. B. Miles
> My Dear Sir,
> I hope you were able to arrange for the meeting in Springfield, and found the City Hall free for *Friday* evening. I feel a little concerned lest you may have adopted a suggestion of mine to have the meeting on

---

[23] John Hemmenway, *Memoir of William Ladd, Apostle of Peace,* with an Introduction by Elihu Burritt (Boston, 1877).

Thursday instead of *Friday* evening. I forgot at the time I made this suggestion, that I had been invited to attend a wedding of one of our neighbors on Thursday evening, and I cannot be away on that evening. So I hope you have not engaged the hall and announced the meeting for that evening. If you have, will you kindly get some one to speak in my place? I think Amasa Walker will do it readily, and he would draw better than I should in Springfield,—for he is very popular there. Then you will have Hon. Francis Gillette of Hartford. So if I am not with you, it will make no difference with the audience, as to number or interest of the meeting to them. But if you have taken the hall for *Friday* evening, it is all right for me, and (D. V) I will be with you.

I think we have very good reason to be satisfied with our Hartford meeting. It made a deep impression on the most influential men in Hartford; and a good deal of talk the next day. I send you a copy of the *Evening Post*, which notices the meeting very favorably. They were all much interested in the music as well as speeches. I suppose Mr Whittlesey will be writing to you today and will tell you how we had to manage to pay the use of the hall, by borrowing $15. I had not money enough with me to do it, nor at home either, for my expenses to Boston and for our Hartford meeting have been about $40. As Mr Whittlesey is virtually a poor man, I made him my guest, paying all but his railway fares. But I have not the slightest doubt that the means will be forthcoming when the public see what we are doing.

Such meetings as those at Boston & Hartford will sow the seed for a harvest that shall pay other meetings and operations. It is singular we should have hit upon the only wet day and night in a whole fortnight. Our singers from New Britain had to go to the *depots* in a carriage, which much increased their expense. I paid $11 in all for them, and $1 for the moving to and fro of the instrument they used. I advanced to Mr. Whittlesey for the hall $10. Should you send the $25 we paid, I wish you would send me the $10 I advanced, and $15 to him to pay what we borrowed. I am quite cleaned out of funds for the present. Also if you feel free to send me the $1. I paid for the instrument, it would lessen the burden on me. For then the meeting will have cost me about $16. I hope Mr. Whittlesey will be in Springfield a day or two before the meeting, to beat up recruits for the platform & audience.

Yours Sincerely
Elihu Burritt

MS. LETTERS FROM ELIHU BURRITT
American Peace Society

New Britain, Ct. Oct. 16/71

Rev J. B. Miles

My Dear Sir,

I hope you feel much gratified at the result of our meeting in Springfield. I think we have good reason to regard it a success. The Arsenal is an iceberg that overhangs and chills the city, and makes an atmosphere unfavorable to Peace. But though the papers treated us very shabbily and tried to ignore the meeting, or put it on the level of a small incident among their local items, it made a deep impression on all present, as we learned next day.— Now we are in for this series of demonstrations we must go ahead, even at some special cost. We are sowing the seed for reaping a harvest of help after this Chicago calamity [24] is a little put back from the front. I am confident that $500 could not be better spent for the cause than in such public meetings from Boston & Washington, and if your treasury is empty for this expenditure, could not the Society *borrow* that amount?—I think it would be very well to hold one of our meetings in *New Bedford* soon, for there are rich Quak-

[24] The great fire.

ers there who would be stirred up to contribute generously to this special movement. We shall incur but small expense at New Haven and Norwich. Now you will probably go on to New Haven on Saturday by first train, and perhaps preach there on Sunday morning for some pulpit. As our meeting in Norwich is on the following Wednesday, would it not be well for you to go on to New York on Monday and prepare the way for a meeting there say in the second week in November You will be very near to N. Y., and it would hardly pay to return from New Haven to Boston before our Norwich meeting. While in New York you could easily run over to Newark and arrange a meeting there perhaps the second day after the New York meeting; for when we begin our Southern *foray*, it would be well to finish it up straight forward, holding a meeting every other day. I think Mr Whittlesey would arrange efficiently beyond New York on to Washington.—I will write today to David A Wells,[25] asking him to take part in our Norwich meeting on the 25th. I am confident all will go well there, especially if Mr Whittlesey & myself go on the day before.—[manuscript torn]

Worcester anymore prominently than you do yourself and others on the bills. They know all about me in Worcester better than anyone outside can tell them. So let me beg you not to announce me as the "learned Blacksmith," or by any other name than simply Elihu Burritt. I am not a blacksmith now, but a literary man, as much so as Dr Holland or anyone else. To call me a *blacksmith* is to revive an association that has been past and gone for 30 years, and it sounds strained and *ad eptandum*. There is but one Elihu Burritt living, and when the name is announced, every .

MS. LETTERS FROM ELIHU BURRITT
American Peace Society

---

[25] David A. Wells (1828-1898), economist and advocate of free trade.

New Britain, Oct 19/71

Rev J. B Miles.

My Dear Sir.

I am quite astonished to hear that "the boot is on the other leg"—that the Society owes Mr Lord [26] for borrowed money instead of his owing the Society. Can it be possible that he really loaned the Society so much money? or is it for service? I hope you may call in some sharp, practical business man to look into these accounts—to see what has been collected under Mr. Lord's administration, and what paid out and for what. Certainly nothing for public meetings, not for an anniversary meeting last spring.

You yourself cannot burden your mind with these things, but some keen bookkeeper or accountant should be put to the work. I hope we shall be able to go on with these meetings—they will bring in money to the treasury as well as give the cause a power it has never had in this country. Could you not make an especial appeal in the Nov. Advocate for funds to carry on these meetings; say for $500 If this appeal does not raise the amount, then could not the Society borrow $500 on a note endorsed by two or three men of our circle? We must go on with them, for they are a great success and a power to move the public. If you cannot raise the money in Boston, I will join Amasa Walker in raising it elsewhere.

I think a meeting in New Bedford will bring in funds, and if you conclude to go there after Worcester, I am ready. I think we shall have a grand meeting in New Haven.

Yours truly

Elihu Burritt

MS. LETTERS FROM ELIHU BURRITT
American Peace Society

---

[26] The Rev. Amasa Lord was the American Peace Society's corresponding secretary and assistant treasurer *pro tem.* from 1870 to 1871.

New Britain, Ct. Oct. 28/71

Rev. J. B. Miles
    My Dear Sir:

Our letters crossed again. It is very well to postpone the Worcester meeting to the 10th. We shall not be able to have a meeting next week I fear. I do not know anyone in Providence who will go ahead. Does not Mr Emery know someone? I thought he was once settled there. If so, he could help arrange for a meeting.

I am glad you approve of the circular and hope you will send it out at once and see what it will bring in. After this Chicago calamity subsides we may go on easily. I wish however we could get up a great meeting in New York. We shall probably get up meetings in Waterbury and Middletown in the next fortnight.

Yours sincerely,
Elihu Burritt

MS. LETTERS FROM ELIHU BURRITT
American Peace Society

New Britain, Nov 7/71

Rev J B. Miles.
    My Dear Sir.

This is a break in our chain of engagements but we must mend it the best we can. But I fear there is another disarrangement we must provide for. Mr Whittlesey and myself thought it safe to arrange meetings in this vicinity *all next* week, including the *15nth*. We thought that next week would be quite free, while waiting for the New York meeting, so we have prepared for three and perhaps four meetings, which we expect will be very fully [attended]

Sunday evening	12	New Britain	
Wednesday "	15	Bristol	
Thursday "	*16*	*Waterbury*	
Sunday "	19	Middletown perhaps	

Now let me beg you not to announce me at Providence for the 15nth. You can well fill up an hour by yourself, and Dr Caswell [?] and others will occupy the rest, and you will have a grand meeting. But if you have not absolutely fixed upon the 15nth, I will be with you the next week, when perhaps we may go to New Bedford the next evening. I will write to Amasa Walker & others of my friends to say the Worcester meeting is postponed

Yours Truly

Elihu Burritt

MS. LETTERS FROM ELIHU BURRITT
American Peace Society

New Britain, Ct. Nov 15/71

Rev J. B. Miles

My Dear Sir

Although Mr Whittlesey has been with me today and written you from my desk, I send you a few lines in addition. We had a grand meeting here last Sunday evening, many of our people think the most interesting we have had in this town ever. To myself personally it was very peculiarly gratifying, as Mr Whittlesey and myself are natives of the place and Mr Buck our resident Methodist minister. A very deep impression has been made, and I think it will be lasting and generous. I think we have enlisted in Mr. Buck a powerful advocate for our cause. His fervid eloquence, forcible thoughts and impressive elocution fit him for a most successful platform orator. I hope you will forward as soon as you can the two certificates of Life membership Mr Whittlesey writes for.

Now as I have paid a considerable sum of money out of my own pocket for the cause in the last two months, I should like the Society to recognise it by sending a few Peace Advocates to persons here, who have expressed a lively interest in the cause. Mr W and myself, thought you might make it a rule to send a copy for a year to every person

who subscribes & pays $5 to the society, though it be to
constitute his pastor life member of the Society. Of course
you will send to Life Members. I enclose a list of names
which I think had best be sent all in one package to the
P. O. or separately in a band to each person. If sent in a
packet of course the name of each person would be written
on his copy. This will be better than to send a packet to any
one person to distribute, for he would drop them into the
post-office, and there would be some delay.

We expect now to hold a meeting in Litchfield on Monday next, at Middletown on Wednesday. On Thursday I
intend to start for Worcester, stopping that night at N.
Brookfield with Mr Walker. I hope this time the weather
and all will be favorable. I am waiting to hear about your
meeting in Providence, and will not make any more arrangements for Connecticut, until I hear what day you
have fixed upon for that city.

Shall I write to Peter Cooper [27] about having his Institute for a meeting in New York? Perhaps he would like to
show his sympathy with this Treaty movement.

Do you wish a page from me for the Dec. Advocate?
I suppose you will insert my last Dew Drop in your Angel
of Peace. I hope this new periodical will be got up taste-
fully and take well.

Yours Truly & Ever
Elihu Burritt

MS. LETTERS FROM ELIHU BURRITT
American Peace Society

New Britain, Ct. Nov. 17/71

Rev J. B. Miles,

My Dear Sir

I am truly in a fix. Not hearing from you
as to the day for the Providence meeting, we have got one

---

[27] Peter Cooper (1791-1883), New York manufacturer and philanthropist,
and founder of Cooper Institute for "the advancement of science and art."

in Middletown for the *same* evening. I greatly regret this in every way. But as you have already postponed one on my account, I must be with you this time. I have written to Hon. Francis Gillette of Hartford, asking him to take my place, and hope he and Mr. Whittlesey, with local help, will fill the time effectively.

But we must be careful in working from two centres hereafter, unless we divide our forces, and go forth in two bands. Now if you wish it, I will correspond with Peter Cooper about having the Institute for a public meeting, with the view of getting it a reduced price. But it will require some canvassing and personal work to get up a good meeting in New York. Now cannot you get off for ten days about the 1st of Dec. and get up the meetings in New York, Princeton, Phila. Wilmington & Baltimore? If we hold these meetings we should go straight forward with them one after the other, with no more than a day between each two. For you could not go back to Boston between them. You will have to bring your writing with you for the Jan. Advocate. You would find a good place for writing in the Astor Library. Will you consider this? If you cannot do it personally, what should you say to Mr. Whittleseys going on and preparing the meetings all the way to Washington? You speak of bringing out the December Advocate in a few days. Would it not be well to issue it say the last day of the month? for it would be well to give a full report of our meetings in it, including Providence & Worcester.

I enclose two pieces cut from the N. Y. World, from which you might quote effectively in your speeches. Please drop me a line on Monday to say where the meeting is to be in Providence

Yours Truly & Ever
Elihu Burritt

MS. LETTERS FROM ELIHU BURRITT
American Peace Society

New Britain, Conn. Nov. 8/71

Gerrit Smith Esq

My Dear Friend.

It has been a long time since we exchanged letters, or met face to face. But I am sure we have held each other in kind remembrance. I have read your letters & communications in the press, and felt I was still *en rapport* with you. I have now been back in the U. S. above a year, having sojourned abroad 7-$\frac{1}{2}$ years this last time. What events we have witnessed in the last ten years! Among the best is this *Washington Treaty*.[28] We are trying to impress this on the public mind by a series of public meetings from Boston to Washington. We have already held ten of them, and they have been very successful. We now propose to go on to New York, Phila. Wilmington, Baltimore & Washington.

The treasury of the Am. Peace Society is "as dry as a contribution box," and we have to depend upon such contributions as we can pick up on the way to pay for halls etc. I have paid out considerable money in this special effort already, but am anxious to see it accomplished to the extent of our programme. I think I shall advance $150.00 as a loan to the Society for the remaining meetings, hoping they will be able to pay it back after awhile. This Chicago calamity bars the way against contributions to the cause at present. I am sure you sympathise fully with this movement, and I have thought that possibly you might be disposed to join me in sustaining it. If you would lend the Society $100, we could finish off these public meetings very efficiently, and I think the series would leave a deeper impression on the public mind in favor of peace than all the other efforts of the Peace Society for twenty years have done.

I hope you are enjoying your usual good health, and

---

[28] The Washington Treaty provided for the arbitration of the *Alabama* Claims.

that your Indian summer of life is full of hope and comfort.

Ever Truly Yours
Elihu Burritt

GERRIT SMITH MILLER COLLECTION
Syracuse University

New Britain, Ct. Nov 28/71

Rev. J. B. Miles
My Dear Sir,

I have just got a very cordial letter from Abram Hewitt, son-in-law of Peter Cooper, saying we may have their Great Hall on the 13. 14. 15. 18 19 or 20th of December and at the lowest price. $50. This is very reasonable. Now what say you to *Monday*, Dec 18? This would leave us time to prepare for all the other meetings Southward. I think we can get gratuitous notices in the N. Y. papers sufficient to draw an audience; and collect enough at the door to pay most of the hall rent. Now if you say the 18nth will you write immediately to Mr Hewitt, taking the hall for that evening; or shall I engage it for the Society? Please drop me a line at once on this point, for there is no time to lose.

When you have settled upon the evening for New York, we will go on to arrange the meetings in Newark Phila. Wilmington, Baltimore & Washington, finishing them all in 8 or 10 days. If you leave these arrangements with Mr. Whittlesey & myself, we will see that they are made in the best manner, so that they shall not take you away from the Advocate.

I am inclined to think Presid. Crosby [29] would be the most eligible man for our chairman in New York. Shall we ask David A. Wells to speak? We ought to make him the Richard Cobden of America in this movement. As soon as you de-

---

[29] Howard Crosby (1826-1891), Presbyterian clergyman, classical scholar and Chancellor of the University of the City of New York.

cide on the evening for New York, we will begin to canvass for influential men to attend. I know some Quakers there in Phila. whom I will write to on the subject. If they will turn out strong they will give strength & the "sinews of war" beside.

When the R. I. Peace Society send you their contribution, I should like to receive the balance of my expenses to & fro, which will be $8 besides what you let me have

Yours Truly & Ever
Elihu Burritt

MS. LETTERS FROM ELIHU BURRITT
American Peace Society

New Britain, Dec. 4 1871.

Rev J. B. Miles

My Dear Sir

I have not yet been to the P. O. and know not if a letter from you is there. But we must now write very often to each other about the meetings. I have written to Rev Dr McCosh, Princeton, to ask if he will preside if we can get up a meeting there *Thursday the 21st*, the day after our New York meeting.

I have also written to Phila. Wilmington & Baltimore to enquire about halls & cooperation. Now the programme I propose is this:

New York	Wednesday,	Dec. 20
Princeton	Thursday	" 21
Philadelphia	Friday	" 22
Wilmington,	Monday	" 25
Baltimore	Tuesday	" 26
Washington	Wednesday	" 27

This is the best we can possibly do in the time. It will make hard work for us; but travelling expenses are heavy and our time is precious. So if you think you can stand this effort, I am willing to try it. I will do all I can by writing, but I think to make the meetings effective, it would be well to send on Mr Whittlesey and let him work them up as he did the New Haven meeting. We will always take a collection for the cause at the end of each meeting, and perhaps we shall raise half our expenses in that way. I hope Gerrit Smith will advance a little money for this special movement as a loan; but if not, I think it may come from some other sources. Now we are committed to the New York meeting anyway. Have you written to Howard Crosby and Dr Tyng [30] to speak at it? If not, will you do it forthwith? I have not heard yet from David A. Wells, but if he should not be with us, we can occupy the time well with Dr Crosby.

Please write without fail to say if you accept this programme, or part of it. Will we go as far as *Phila.* if no further? You remember Dr Malcolm has promised $50 for a meeting there. If we cannot raise the means to go further we will stop at Phila.

Of course you will have time to get out the Jan. Advocate before the 20th Hope you will devote one page or more to our meetings, and will you be careful to direct the full names of subscribers to be given to their contributions? I hope the Dec. Advocate is now going out to subscribers

Yours Truly & Ever

Elihu Burritt

MS. LETTERS FROM ELIHU BURRITT
American Peace Society

New Britain, Conn. Dec. 7/71

Hon. Gerrit Smith

My Dear Friend,

I thank you most sincerely for your good and kind letter, and for your generous contribution to our special movement to promote the cause of peace through the text of the Washington Treaty. Your gift will be very helpful. I am going to assume the pecuniary responsibility

---

[30] Dr. Stephen H. Tyng (1800-1885), rector of St. George's Church, New York City.

of the New York Meeting, hoping the Society may pay me back when it obtains funds. I feel sad that you talk and feel as if you were an *old* man. I cannot realize it of you or myself. I feel young in heart and hope, but to-morrow is my *sixty-first* birthday! What our hands find to do we must do quickly. How hard to realise ourselves so near the end of our course! If one were young now what obvious changes for the better he [manuscript torn]—I think I sent you a pamphlet containing several of these articles on "The Eastern and Western Questions of Europe." I am now writing papers for the N. Y. *Independent* on Labor, Banking & other questions, especially the bearing of an inflated credit currency on the business and interests of the country.

I am glad you are as active as ever in the Temperance cause. What gateways to destruction these liquor shops prove all the world over. In England they swallow up full one third of the wages of laboring men and swallow up something more valuable still. I wish you every success in your great movement.

I hope to see you again face to face to renew the experiences of the past. How much cheaper would compensated Emancipation have been than the emancipation wrought out by the sword!

GERRIT SMITH MILLER COLLECTION
Syracuse University

New Britain, Conn Dec. 7/71

Rev J. B. Miles
　My Dear Sir
　　I have just written to Mr. Hewitt to ask if we can have the Cooper Institute on Monday or Tuesday instead of Wednesday the 20th; I think it probable that the change can be made; but if not, we must go on with the 20th and do the best we can as to speakers or chairman. Will you write to Dr. Stephen H. Tyng, asking him to speak? And would it

not be well to ask Wm Cullen Bryant also to speak? He will represent the press and literature, and speak noble sentiments that will find an echo abroad. With Dr Crosby, Tyng, and Bryant, you and I could occupy the time pretty well. I will perhaps telegraph you on Saturday if I get a reply from New York, so no time may be lost, for we have none to lose.

I have received a cordial letter from Dr McCosh, Princeton, expressing much sympathy with our cause, but saying that all the students will be off for their Christmas holidays in that week. So I write by this post to Rev Dr Stearns Newark, to ask if he will open his church for us on Thursday evening, the 21. Will also write to Phila. to ask if we can have the Music Hall there on *Friday* evening 22. We must try to go as far as Phila. if no further.

I enclose draft of the letter inviting influential men to attend the meeting. As soon as the date is fixed, you had better print it and send to as many influential men in New York as you can get names; of course to all the editors. I am sorry about the necessity of changing the evening for the time is short. Please write me often.

Yours Truly & Ever
Elihu Burritt

MS. LETTERS FROM ELIHU BURRITT
American Peace Society

New Britain, Ct Dec. 23/71

Rev J. B. Miles

My Dear Sir

I have a letter from W. M. White, of Amherst, saying that we may have the College Hall any evening after Jan. 11. Now suppose we get up a meeting at the same time at East Hampton, and see if we cannot impress Samuel Williston, the great millionaire & philanthropist. Perhaps he will give you $100 or more. Suppose we say Wednesday, Jan 17 for Amherst and Thursday 18, for East Hampton? If you agree to this, will you write in a day or two to Rev. Dr. Seeley, East Hampton, asking him if he will open his church to us on the 18nth? I think he will do it readily. Then we must be sure to have Mr Williston present to hear our arguments, as he may be favorably impressed and inclined to open his purse. I will save out these two days from engagements we are making in Connecticut for meetings. Before we go to Phila. & South we must raise some funds. I hope you will not be discouraged by small pecuniary success in N. Y. Our sowing there may bring some sheaves yet. Since you came to the helm more has been done to make the Peace cause a movement than was done before for 25 years. I feel that you owe it to yourself and the cause to take a firm and decided stand; that a rigid examination should be instituted into Mr Lords' administration, to ascertain how much money came into his hands, what he did with it and how he ran the Society into such debt. To my view there is something suspicious about his administration. I suppose that the Advocate contains the contributions received while he held the Secretariat; what was paid for rent, office work and for printing, bills must show. I hope you will also think of our conversation at the Bible House, whether the Society cannot be *nationalised* by locating it in N. Y.—It is now a *local*, Boston organization in name. Please excuse my repeated references to this subject, for you will understand my motive.

Yours Sincerely,
Elihu Burritt

MS. LETTERS FROM ELIHU BURRITT
American Peace Society

New Britain, Ct. Dec. 30/71.

Rev J. B. Miles
 My Dear Sir
    Our young friend W. M. White of Amherst called yesterday and I had a long talk with him and posted him about the Treaty, and urged him to expand his paper into an address for the platform, after reading it, and come into the

cause as an advocate. He is deeply interested in the cause. He says *Monday* evening Jan. 15 is the best evening for our meeting at Amherst; and will fix and prepare it for that time. This will be good economy of time for us. I think I will write to Hon. Samuel Williston, East Hampton, to try to prepare his mind for the meeting and his purse too. We must get $100 out of him at least. I have a cousin in East Hampton, whom I shall stay with probably.

Mr Whittlesey came up from N. H to see me the other day. I persuaded him to hold on to the cause in which he becomes more and more interested. I told him the funds would come in after this Chicago disaster had passed off. He has a little promised him in New Haven after New Years. I gave him $10 to prepare for meetings. It is absolutely necessary that one from us should go personally, for we can depend upon no *local* help to get up a meeting. We have two meetings appointed for next week; at Meriden, Wednesday, Wallingford Thursday; probably the 10nth & 11th at Bridgeport and Norwalk. We shall endeavor to get up two meetings a week in Connecticut through the winter. I hope you will raise up some earnest men to go out with you, so we may have two bands in the field; to make a good report in the Advocate. If we have churches, a collection will perhaps pay our expenses. How should you be disposed to insert my Olive Leaf that first appears in the London Peace Herald? It may interest some of the readers.

Yours Truly & Ever
Elihu Burritt

MS. LETTERS FROM ELIHU BURRITT
American Peace Society

New Britain, Ct. Feb. 5/72

Rev J. B. Miles,
  My Dear Friend
  I am under a cloud of gloom just now, as my eldest sister lies at the point of death. I have just written to Mr Whit-

t!esey to postpone the meetings this week to the next. So I
cannot write fully to you now. I am afraid there is to be a
break-down in the Treaty. Our Political partisans or our
political Government has put too much *Buncombe* for home
consumption in this *Casc*—an *Irish price* which they know
the Court will not allow, but which may operate on politics
here. There is too much of Charles Sumner's programme in
it. Still, we must stick to the Treaty, and I am ready to do
what I can. I think it would be well for you to ask Dr
Stearns [31] of Amherst to write a few lines to his brother in
Newark to testify to the character of our meetings, as suit-
able to his Church. Then a letter from you to Dr Stearns
of Newark, asking him for the church I think would be successful. We could go to Princeton the next evening and on
to Phila. But I will write more fully when I emerge from
this bereavement impending on our family. We should have
plenty of time to arrange at all the chief cities, and I hope
our Treaty text will not be nullified by a repudiation of it
by England. I do think our claim for indirect losses preposterous, and a violation of both the letter & spirit of the
Treaty, and that the claim is merely electioneering Buncombe. But it may all blow over. I will write soon again

      Yours Ever
      Elihu Burritt

MS. LETTERS FROM ELIHU BURRITT
American Peace Society

        New Britain, Feb. 8/72

Rev J. B. Miles
 My Dear Friend.
  Although we buried our dear Sister yesterday, I felt
constrained even by my sense of what her wish would be, to go
straight from the funeral to Waterbury, where a public
meeting had been announced and prepared for the evening.

---

[31] The Rev. William Augustus Stearns (1805-1876) was at this time president of Amherst College.

It could not be postponed and I felt bound to fulfil the duty taken upon me. I have just returned; and we had one of the very best meetings of our series. Mr Whittlesey did better than I ever heard him, especially on the present phase of the Treaty, or the excitement in England. I still feel that it was most undignified, unfair and most unwise for our Government to put in to the Case claims which they knew no impartial Court would admit for a moment, but which, when rejected, as they must be, would leave a sense of surrender on the part of our people. I feel that our Supreme Court at Washington, would have rejected these outside, vague and inappreciable claims. I look upon them as Charles Sumner's Buncombe speech injected into the Treaty. I admire his genius and spirit, but I always felt he argued the case like a Philadelphia lawyer, and that war would have been inevitable if his views had been enforced. This setting an Irish price with the view of reducing it in trade to an honest standard does not comport in my view with the dignity of a great nation.

But these exaggerated claims prove the necessity of an impartial Court of Arbitration, and if such a court sifts the chaff out of them, it will be a triumph of justice & peace. Mr Whittlesey is arranging for two meetings next week in Norwalk and Danbury. Have you really fixed upon the New Bedford meeting? Please let me know soon definitely, so that we may not clash in our meetings.

I notice that you give no receipt of monies collected at our Connecticut meetings. Mr Whittlesey says he has twice forwarded you the amounts, but they have not been acknowledged in the Advocate. I fear this may make an unfavorable impression on its readers in these towns we have visited— that they may think Mr Whittlesey does not account for the money he receives. Do please see to this in next Advocate. It might be well to enter the collections as received by him as Agent for Connecticut.

The last No was the best you have issued; quite *international* in its contributions. I am writing to some interesting writers in England to contribute short bits for the *Angel*. Hope you get it into Sunday Schools as an interesting monthly.

Yours Truly & Ever

Elihu Burritt

P. S. I think we must take Baltimore & Wilmington on our way back from Washington, arranging for the meetings there as we go on south. If England should withdraw from the Treaty, of course our occupation is gone in the way of these meetings.

MS. LETTERS FROM ELIHU BURRITT
American Peace Society

New Britain, Ct. Feb. 13/72

Rev. J. B Miles.

My Dear Sir

This unfortunate excitement about the Treaty, it seems to me, must modify our course a little, about Washington especially. I fear our usual Addresses would be out of date and out of court there. I still hope and believe that the Treaty stand and that the Court will fully riddle the wheat out of the chaff of "Our Case". I will hold myself ready to go on with you say *Thursday* of next week if you like. We might have a meeting on that evening at Newark and the next evening at Princeton, if they can be got up, but if not, we can take them on our way back. Perhaps you might arrange with Dr Stearns: to have a meeting Thursday or Friday evening of next week. Then we could stop over part of a day in Phila. and arrange there for a meeting on our return. But we must decide immediately. I leave it all with you. Write me when we shall start. I think, however, we had better have *one* meeting at least on our way to Washington, at Newark or Princeton. I will write to Ashur Clarke,

Baltimore, to ask if a Church would be open to us there on Monday evening, the 26th.

I have sent a pretty vigorous article to the N. Y. World, giving my views of "Consequential damages"; it will be out to-morrow; and you will see what view I take of the policy of an *Irish price*.

I enclose a piece I wrote a few years ago illustrating the Law of Kindness. It may be too long for the Angel, but perhaps would do for the Advocate.

I thank you for your sympathy with me in this sudden bereavement. It was hard to perform the duty at Waterbury but I went through it comfortably

Yours Truly & Ever

Elihu Burritt

P. S. I send all I have, except a few copies of my tract. I wish Mr Dunham would have them counted as I have not time. Also enclose a few of my pamphlets.

MS. LETTERS FROM ELIHU BURRITT
American Peace Society

New Britain, April 8, /72

[The Rev. J. B. Miles]
My Dear Friend

I return Dr Peabodys [32] letter. I hope it will not affect your mind at all in regard to the Congress. Of course, we must expect about half of those we write to will decline to sign the Call. I would keep all the letters, and every scrap relating to the Congress. Will you send me two or three copies of the Call, for I should like to write to Henry Richard next Friday and should like to enclose one to him, so that he may have time to write an article on it in the May Herald.[33] Perhaps you had better write also. Do write me often.

[32] Dr. Andrew Preston Peabody (1811-1893), Unitarian clergyman of Boston, college professor and author

[33] *The Herald of Peace* was the organ of the London Peace Society.

I go to New Haven tomorrow, and expect to speak at Guilford & Clinton on Wednesday & Thursday evenings

Yours Ever

Elihu Burritt

MS. LETTERS FROM ELIHU BURRITT
American Peace Society

Hartford, Conn. April 24, 1872.

[The Rev. J. B. Miles]

My Dear Friend:

I fear I was too fidgety and unintelligible this morning about the Congress; and I send you a few lines from here in regard to my views. I feel that we have fully put our hand to the plow and cannot and must not look back; that everything is favorable as to time and circumstances; that if we are to have the Congress *this* year, we shall lose precious time by leaving the time indefinite. Everyone who attends from abroad will want to know as soon as possible the exact time, so as to prepare accordingly. Whoever wishes to write papers to be read will need to know the exact time, that he may measure his work. So we shall lose more working time on *this* end than we shall gain on the other by postponing or leaving the date unsettled. Now as we agreed so fully upon it at New Bedford, and have issued our circular, let us by all mean go ahead on that line. If you and I are perfectly agreed, we can bring all the rest to our decision. A few must act decisively in such matters. A multitude of counsellors confuse action Now my view is: That you write to David A. Wells, Norwich, Longfellow & Whittier for their signatures, and if you can get them, put the names forthwith upon the Circular and go to press with say 500 or 1000 as soon as possible. You will have a good array of representative names, well known abroad. As soon as they are ready I will help you get up a list of English and Continental names to address, so that such letters may be posted from this side.

Then we will commence writing special letters to special jurists, publicists etc, pressing a strong invitation for them to attend. If you will send me 100 of the Calls I will write to persons I know a letter to go with the printed paper. Not a day is to be lost in getting out the invitation. Even if you get no more names, let those go out that you have. I hope and believe you will be able to get David A. Wells. I have written him to say that we hope he will be the Richard Cobden in the Congress.

As soon as we have posted the Circulars to those we wish to attend, then you an I must go on to New York and get up there a local Committee of Arrangements, for the reception of guests, for their courteous welcome and entertainment etc. We must see Peter Cooper and see if we can have the Institute without charge. We will also wait upon wealthy men to obtain a guarantee fund & subscriptions for the *expenses.*

Now as to money. The Congress must not draw from your Society or from its regular contributors. We must milk another cow altogether. So will you please open up a separate account for Congress expenses, to even a sheet of paper used?

The printing and postage up to the assembling of the Congress will cost about $100. The printing during the Congress will probably cost $100 more. So the bill will not be very heavy until Congress meets. If we get the Institute for nothing, then I think $500 will cover all expenses, exclusive of the volume which may be published of the speeches, resolutions and proceedings. Your Society must be paid for all the extra work you provide. You and I must carry on the correspondence chiefly.

Now then, my life and health are precarious; but if am spared till the Congress I will guarantee $500 toward the necessary expenses, with the understanding that I may have a little direction as to their application. When wealthy influential men see that we are in earnest, that we have actually issued invitations to hundreds of distinguished men in Europe, they will come forward with ample means.

It is very necessary that you and I, if we are to act as joint secretaries, shall be in frequent communication. We ought at least to write to each other twice a week. I feel very deeply interested in your own position and prospects, fearing you may become discouraged. The Society was hub deep in the mire when you took hold. A great deal of obloquy had to be overcome. People everywhere seem apathetic and even niggardly in their support. But we have sown a good deal of seed in this campaign which will bear grain ere long. A Peace Congress would be worth $5000 a year to your Society.

It would be a great fact that would put the Society on a new footing before the country. So go on with full faith & hope. I feel so strongly about this Congress that I should not shrink from guaranteeing the whole expense rather than it should fail, and I am ready to begin to foot the printing & postage bills forthwith, if funds do not come in for it. But as soon as we can say that we have issued the Invitations, we will draw up a special appeal for funds for the Congress.

Now I expect to hear from you twice a week.

Yours Faithfully
Elihu Burritt

MS. LETTERS FROM ELIHU BURRITT
American Peace Society

New Britain, Conn., May 10, 1872

Dear Charles Sumner,

I thank you for your kind and frank letter. I have indeed labored many years for Arbitration, and no man in this country rejoiced with more hope and faith than I did at the consummation of the Washington Treaty. I have at over 30 public meetings endeavored to convey a sense of my appreciation of this event; and have done the same in many letters to public journals. I regard it as going beyond all former treaties, as it laid down the fundamental rules which all nations must accept even if the Geneva Court breaks down.[34] I consider the concession of England in consenting to these retroactive rules as an unparalleled act in the history of nations. But although I have sought for such terms, I have not found any sufficiently expressive to convey my sense of the dishonor put upon our nation by presenting claims which no one at home or abroad believes to be honest or sincere. I cannot modify any views I have expressed by tongue or pen on that subject. I know if the case were reversed, we should feel, say and do what England does now. We repudiated the arbitration of the King of the Netherlands in regard to our North-Eastern boundary on a ten times less ground.[35]

In a word, the Treaty and Court are the grandest transactions in the history of nations; but I feel our case is dishonorable to both; that it was given to the sharp cunning of a Philadelphia lawyer to construct, and that parts of it bring shame upon the cheeks of millions of our countrymen of all parties. There is no part of it that so unpleasantly affects my sense of honor, dignity, & propriety as the effort to turn this noble & patriotic Cobden into states evidence against his own country, and make his generous speeches part of the indictment against it. How should we feel if Bismarck should do the same by you, and make a case against us for "consequential damages," adopting your speeches on the French arms scandal as his *brief?* Would such a liability tend to raise the tone of national morality, and freedom of utterance in Parliament or Congress?

I feel exceedingly anxious about your relation to this great difficulty. I know that nine in ten in England regard you as the author of these consequential claims, which bar

---

[34] John H. Latané, *A History of American Foreign Policy* (N. Y., 1934), pp. 208–209.

[35] SUMNER MSS., *Letters Received*, Vol. CXXX. Harvard College Library.

the way to a fair & satisfactory settlement. I fear nearly the same proportion of the community here adopt the same view. I was in England when you made your great speech, and I think you have never been able to realize the deep & unhappy impression it made upon the whole country. Certainly no speech on this continent ever produced such an impression there. As soon as the Treaty was ratified, the friends of peace there set on foot a most vigorous movement in favor of Arbitration.[36] They raised nearly £1000 [?] to support it. They held 70 public meetings a week to that end. Henry Richard, M. P.,[37] my old colleague, was to bring a motion before Parliament this session. But *our* case bars the way,[38] and he and thousands interested in his motion are distressed and mortified. He wrote me a few weeks ago asking me if we could not do something towards removing the obstruction. He said that one of the hardest things for him and the friends of peace to bear was the thought that you, to whom they had looked with such hope and faith, were the author of this difficulty. I have felt you might not realize how your relation to this case is regarded in England,[39] and I hope you will pardon this frankness on my part, and that you will do what you can to overcome this hitch, and to restore you to the old love and admiration of your best friends abroad, and which I have never lost.

Ever and faithfully Yours,
Elihu Burritt.

SUMNER MSS., *Letters*, Vol. CXII

[36] *Herald of Peace,* Vol. XIII n s. (Jan. 1, 1873), p. 5.
[37] C. Miall, *Henry Richard, M. P* (London, 1889).
[38] Richard's motion was introduced and carried on July 9, 1873.
[39] Sumner was, as a matter of fact, constantly receiving letters of protest from his friends and acquaintances in England.

Senate Chamber

1st June '72

My dear Burritt,

I enclose resolutions which I hope you will not dislike. Devoted to peace & to Arbitration as a substitute for War, I have seen with regret the movement in England to dishonor this cause, as it seems to me. Even our friends of the Peace Society have yielded to the political pressure, reminding me of the old saying at Venice—*Veneziani primò é por Christiani.*

It seems to me that our only [hope] is to insist upon *Arbitrate* as a substitute for war. Will you think kindly of this?

Ever Sincerely Yours,

Charles Sumner

BURRITT MSS.

Library of the Institute of New Britain

New Britain, Conn. Dec. 24/72.

Rev J. B. Miles,

My Dear Sir;

I am very sorry indeed that the unfortunate accident I met with on my recent journey prevents me from accompanying you on your mission to Europe. But I have full confidence that you will effect all that could be done if I were with you; and I hope you will go in full faith on this point.

I hope you will carry with you the strong and mutual impression that resulted from our conversation here, that the present is the most favorable juncture the world ever saw for making a great movement to establish permanent and universal peace; that this new year should not be allowed to pass by without such a movement to distinguish it above all the years this generation has witnessed.

Then, next to this firm and deep impression, let me urge you to maintain the other opinion to which we came, that

this country is the fitting place for such a Congress as we
contemplate. You know how strongly I feel on this point,
and I need not repeat the reasons I have urged in regard
to it. Among the first is this: That it is *our* turn, as a
nation, to assume the *hosthood* of an International Peace
Congress. For four years in succession the American friends
of Peace went first to Brussels, then Paris, Frankfort, and
London to the great congresses held at those capitals. They
did not contribute a single dollar for the heavy expenses involved in each of those congresses. The English friends paid
every farthing of these expenses, and performed all the labor
in organising them. Now I feel it keenly, that it would be
mean and shabby on our part to ask or wish them to do the
same in regard to another Congress, as they would inevitably
have to do, if it were held anywhere else than in this country.
If it were held in London, Paris, Frankfort, Berlin or The
Hague, the English would have to foot all the bills for halls,
circulars tickets, and printed documents. You will remember, I am sure, all the other motives and considerations I
urged in favor of holding the Congress in America. I will
mention only one more:

This country is the most *neutral* in Christendom for such
a Congress and for the elaboration of an International Code.
We have no "entangling alliances" with European nations.
We stand in the most friendly and impartial relations to
them all. Then one great and distinguishing fact fits and
almost entitles us to have the Congress here. The *first* and
only rules of International Law ever adopted and acted upon
by Governmental authority were elaborated *here*, at Washington, by the Joint High Commissioners. These rules are
law, as far as they go, today. The first High Court of
Nations sanctioned [sic] them at Geneva, and no nation
hereafter will dare to set them aside. They cover a considerable space of the ground that a full International Code
must occupy. Thus this country is the very *birth-place* of
International Law, or of the first clauses of it that have

any authority. Will any European power demur to their authority because they were elaborated in this country? Certainly not. Then what country is more fitted for *completing* the entire Code than this?

Then another most auspicious coincidence will favor the holding the Congress here. The meeting of the Evangelical Alliance next October will bring over from Europe eminent men from different countries, who will represent the religious world; who will come for an object in full sympathy and alliance with such a Peace Congress as we propose. A large number of these men, fresh from the brotherly fellowship and communion of a common faith, would come in and take part in its proceedings, and deepen its international character in representation and in spirit.

Then we can offer the generous hospitalities of New York to all the foreign members at least: a pleasure and a duty which we may well ask after having been the guests of English hospitality so often at the Peace Congresses in Europe. Then we can arrange with the Steamship Companies to bring and return them free or at reduced rates.

Now I am anxious that you should press the other and most important point of our programme, which is to make the Congress differ from any one that has yet been held. That is; that we propose to convene *two distinct* bodies, to meet in *different halls* and for *different objects*. That one is to be a great popular Congress, composed perhaps of 2000 members, representing all the Countries of Christendom, embracing men of all professions, parties and denominations, to discuss the whole *morale* of the subject, embracing principle and sentiment, that the other is to be what perhaps we had better call, a SENATE OF JURISTS, numbering 50, 40, or 30 of the first publicists of the world, who shall meet by themselves, not to make or hear speeches, but to sit down together to the elaboration of an International Code, clause by clause, after the manner and in the spirit of the Joint

High Commissioners at Washington, perhaps adopting the three rules adopted by these Commissioners as three of the Clauses of the Code. This *Senate of Jurists* to be composed of just such publicists as their respective Governments would not only be willing but *obliged* to choose if they themselves should inaugurate a Joint High Commission to frame an International Code. I think England has six men who would represent her well, and who are not in official or Governmental positions. At the head of these we may place Sir R. Phillimore with Lord Dentenden, Prof. Bernard, Vernon Harcourt and Prof. Leone Levi.[40] France could furnish an equal number of publicists of equal learning & eminence, and Germany, Italy, Russia and other countries, each a few men of great reputation in International Law. Now then, when, say, *thirty* of such eminent jurists should meet at New York with half a dozen of our first publicists headed by Pres. Woolsey, they would constitute a body which would give the positive authority of *law* to the Code which they should elaborate. They would address themselves to the work with all the sense of responsibility they would feel if they were commissioned to perform it by their own Governments, and the work would be accepted by their Governments and countries as performed for them by the best authorities in the world. When it was finished, great ratification meetings might be held in America & Great Britain, and all other countries in which such meetings are allowed.

To my mind, this SENATE OF JURISTS is to be the great fact and consummation to be aimed at. This will cost the most effort and involve the most care and discretion. It will be an easy matter to get up a Popular Peace Congress of 2000 members in the Cooper Institute, to make eloquent and fervid orations and to listen to them. But to convene, in a small "upper room" or hall, Fifty of the first Jurists of the world will require great care, circumspection and

---

[40] British authorities on jurisprudence.

labor. They will come, if they can be sure to meet as men of equal standing, who shall command the respect and confidence of their Governments and the world at large. For instance, Sir R. Phillimore would want to know what kind of men he would have to associate with in such a Senate. If he were to meet and confer with a *de Tocqueville*, he would feel it an honor to do it. Thus, in inviting European authorities to unite in such a Senate, it would be of great importance to secure the attendance of men as nearly on the same level of standing and reputation as possible. I hope Pres. Woolsey, who is known to them all, and knows them also, will send you the addresses of those who he thinks would best compose such a Senate, and perform its work. I have written to him to this effect, and I hope you will hear from him in a day or two.

In conclusion, if you have no objection to the term, "*Senate of Jurists*," I wish you would use it, to designate and distinguish it always from the great *Peace Congress*, so as always to keep them distinct when they are spoken of.

Now wishing you the best success in your mission, I am Ever & Truly Yours.

Elihu Burritt.

MS. LETTERS FROM ELIHU BURRITT
American Peace Society

New Britain, Connecticut
Dec. 27, 1872.

My Dear Sir

I beg to commend to your courteous and kind consideration the bearer of this note—Rev. J. B. Miles, Secretary of the American Peace Society, who visits Europe for the purpose of conferring with the friends of Peace, and of inviting them to an International Peace Congress in the United States during the coming year. I am sure your interest in the cause will dispose you to aid him in this mission with your hearty sympathy and cooperation; that you will favor the great enterprize which he goes to propose and promote; and that you will assist him in obtaining the active cooperation of others in its behalf. He will fully unfold to you the views and wishes of the friends of Peace in America in regard to the proposed Congress and they hope that the friends of the same cause in Europe will unite with them that the coming year will be a most auspicious time for a great and united effort to abolish war and to establish peace as the permanent and universal condition of the civilized nations.

Yours very truly,
Elihu Burritt.

To

Isaac B. Cooke. Esq., 19 Royal Exchange, Liverpool.
William A. Cunningham, Esq., Bank-Manager, Manchester.
J. B. Gould, Esq., U. S. Consul, Birmingham.
Charles Gilpin, Esq., M. P. 10 Bedford Sq., London.
Benjamin Moran, Esq., Sec. U. S. Legation, London.
Frederic Passy, Sec. Societe des Amis de La Paix, Paris.
Auguste Visschers, Brussels.
Dr. George Varentrap, Frankfort.
M. du Mont-Schauberg, Cologne.
Prof. J. Torold Rogers, Oxford.

MS. LETTERS FROM ELIHU BURRITT
American Peace Society

New Britain, Conn., Dec. 27, 1872

Dear Charles Sumner,

I want to tell you how much I thank you for the magnanimous resolutions [41] you have introduced in regard to the perpetuation and imitation of the sad memories of the past in the battle flags to be flaunted hereafter in the faces of subdued foes with whom we should in those immortal words, "clasp hands over the bloody chasm," which so lately

---

[41] *The Congressional Globe*, 3d session, 42nd Congress, Part I, p. 2 (Washington, 1873). The resolution provided that the names of battles with fellow citizens should not be continued in the *Army Register* or placed on the regimental colors of the United States.

ran so deep with the most precious blood of the nation. You never did anything more completely like yourself than in presenting these resolutions, and I earnestly hope that the remonstrance of "Philip drunk" will not deter you from pressing it to the full adoption in letter and spirit. Perhaps Massachusetts will be sobered to a second and better thought ere long. The Massachusetts that will hold your life, labor, and memory dearest is in its cradle now. It is the posterity that will do justice to your reputation, and no act of your life will it prize as a dearer jewel than this effort of great hearted patriotism, which might gracefully close and crown your political life, if God should will it soon to end.

We cannot afford to have an American "*Boyne Water*," or "*Croppers Lie Down!*" nor any other taunting songs and emblems of discord sung or flaunted by American lips or hands. We cannot afford to pit the *orange* against the *green* in our cities and capitals or influence memories that should "have repentant ashes strewn on their heads," and be buried in sackcloth in the earth. What a Satan among the Sons of God would be the presence of these battle-flags at the great centenary of our Nation's independence in 1876! What would those regiments, that would thus emblazon their battles among the stars of the old flag, say to the places and dates of these bloody conflicts being carved in the Monument of Washington at the National Capital? If they would not venture nor wish to engrave them in that monument, nor unfold them from Independence Hall in 1876, how can they glory in lifting them up in the face of that pure and peaceful heaven which we hope shall forevermore enfold the American Union, with all its happy family of States, in its loving embrace?

Most earnestly do I hope that no criticism nor remonstrance, dictated by a spirit that calls itself patriotism, will deter you from the course you have adopted in your resolutions; that the flag of the Union, laid across "the bloody chasm" to conceal the closing abyss shall not enumerate nor symbolize the many springs and streams that once fed and filled the red flood that gurgled within its jaws. You know as well as any other man what manner of verdict this generation has rendered in regard to sentiments and acts deemed just and honorable in a past age. If other considerations could weigh with you than your own convictions of duty, then you may draw in anticipation upon the approving conscience and verdict of a coming generation, and the application of an ever-present God of justice, to sanction and encourage your effort.

Yours Sincerely & Ever
Elihu Burritt

SUMNER MSS., *Letters Received*, Vol. CXVIII
Harvard College Library

New Britain, June 23, 1873.

[Rev. J. B. Miles]
My Dear Friend:

I hope your third meeting succeeded in bringing the two malcontents to reason, or you to a full determination to go on without them or despite them. There is no time to lose. I suppose you have received several more adhesions to our INTERNATIONAL CODE COMMITTEE—that it now presents a list of influential names representing many states and positions. Now if any difficulty occurs with Pres. Woolsey about signers of the invitation & European Jurists, it strikes me we can do this very properly—we can attach *all* the names of the International Code Committee and you and I sign the note of invitation on their behalf; putting our names first, and giving the names of the Committee afterwards, as if to apprize those we write to whom we represent. This we can do at once, and I think it will obviate all scruples and difficulties that Mr Woolsey or others may feel in regard to prominence or precedence. Perhaps it will also make a better impression abroad, to see who the committee are; as it will look more like complete organization. We can not now retreat or hesitate. The letter of Visscher's must decide the matter and we must move on even if you have to surrender your connection with the Peace Society, which would kill the Society forever. It would no longer have *raison d'etre*—Would it not be well to have Visscher's letter well translated and published with the one we wrote him? I think the correspondence would give the movement an impulse. I would send it to one of the great New York Dailies as the Times, Tribune, or World. Then it will reach the nation entire. Every News Paper in New England is *local* except *Springfield Republican.* I think any one of N. Y. dailies would publish this correspondence.

Write me often, if but a dozen lines at a time. We must now act together, and consider well every step.

Ever Yours,
Elihu Burritt

MS. LETTERS FROM ELIHU BURRITT
American Peace Society

New Britain, June 28—73

[Rev. J. B. Miles]
My dear Friend:

I earnestly hope you will have *back-bone* enough to hold you up stiff and strong through this contest with senseless crotchets. I never knew anything more preposterous than the opposition of members of your *soi-disant* committee to this great and glorious movement, which would lift the Peace Society up to a mighty power in the world, recognized and honored of all men & nations. Let me beg you not to yield an iota, nor be turned aside or back an inch from the course you have committed yourself to. Don't waste another hour in parleying with the malcontents. We cannot lose another hour in such senseless discussions and delay. A *rôle* opens up before you equal and even surpassing Richard Cobden's. Don't be cheated out of it. Throw yourself into the work heart & soul, not a Secretary of the A. P. S. [American Peace Society] but as Secretary of the International Code Committee of America. This movement requires all your time, strength & talents until consummated. Let your next be the final meeting for discussing the question "To be or not to be." If the opposition continues, I hope you will withdraw at once from the Peace Society, as secretary, and throw yourself fully and unreservedly into the Code Mission. You stand pledged to Europe as well as America to go forward in it. It will support you; funds will come in when the movement is fairly launched. I hope a considerable amount has already been subscribed.

You feel as deeply as I that every dollar subscribed for this special Mission should be kept sacred and separate to its object. Now in view of the secession of the Peace Society it is more important than ever that not a dollar should be mixed up with the funds of the Society. Pay the Society for every service rendered by it, for every sheet of paper, stamp, etc., but let the two treasuries be kept rigidly separate. Write me often, for you and I must work together in the closest union in this matter; but we may have to work alone. I will keep Visschers letter for a day or two and think it over.

Ever & Truly Yours,
Elihu Burritt

MS. LETTERS FROM ELIHU BURRITT
American Peace Society

New Britain, July 17/73

[Rev. J. B. Miles]
My Dear Friend

You are progressing nobly. All promises well. Nothing but MONEY can obstruct, and that I am sure will be forthcoming. I suppose you will have seen the N. Y. Times of yesterday, with the correspondence with Visschers. They did not publish my introduction to it as I expected, but I am sure the two letters will explain the movement and impress the public mind. I enclose a letter from Charles Sumner. You will see how he is impressed with Henry Richard's success in Parliament. But you will go on the Continent to do a greater work than he could do. I hope you will get off as soon as possible, to head off or overcome all misdirected operations. You will not swerve an inch from the programme you have fixed upon—a Senate of Jurists at Brussels. I am terribly busy with my building. Must go to Canada next week with our family for rest and recreation. Do write me often—tell me how soon you can get off to Europe. Every moment is precious. I will write again before I leave.

Ever & Truly Yours
Elihu Burritt

MS. LETTERS FROM ELIHU BURRITT
American Peace Society

St. Catharines, Ont., Aug. 16. '73.

[Rev. J. B. Miles]
My Dear Friend:

I received your letter dated Rutland, yesterday, and was very glad to hear from you. I think you have progressed remarkably in every way, and that the movement will be a success that will impress the world. I am glad you went to Albany and have seen Mons. Pruyn.[42] I do not know his standing as an authority, but he occupies a good position. We must press Woolsey to go over. He is the first American in status as an authority—I will write him an earnest letter, if you think it will be of any worth, will also write Lawrence & Pruyn as soon as I return. You do not say if the Circular brings in any money—I hope it does. Our *American* people are very slow in regard to the cause and we shall have to depend upon a very few persons who appreciate the importance of the movement and have the means.

[42] John van Scharck Lansing Pruyn (1811-1877) was a distinguished corporation lawyer, regent and chancellor of the University of the State of New York and member of Congress.

I am sorry almost that I have cramped myself so much by building, which has already exceeded the first estimate. My health is always precarious. My old ailment follows me and sometimes it seems as if my life were going to blow out like a candle in the wind. I long to go over and take part in this great Congress or movement. But I shall have to decide a few days before I start, when I am hopeful and comfortable.

I hope you will write again to Visschers and tell him you are to be in Brussels soon and will cooperate with them in making all necessary preparations. I congratulate you that you can throw your vigorous health & strength into the movement. Now I need not say more about *faith* and *courage*. You will have more to meet with from self-seeking friends like him of Ghent than from open enemies of the cause. If you can bring 25 or 30 jurists of eminence together at Brussels it will be worth the best ambition and energy of a life. I think we must have a grand meeting at the *Hague*.

Now I want to see you greatly before you leave. Will you sail from New York? or will you not be again in New London? If so I can meet you on the way, even if you cannot pass through New Britain I cannot well diverge to Boston on my way back, as we shall be a large company with much luggage. Of course you will visit New London again before you leave, and then we can arrange to meet.

We remain here until next week Saturday the 24th, when we go on to Toronto & spend two or three days. Intend to be at home by the 28th or 29th.

If you can write me by *Wednesday* next, please direct to me here. On the Thursday of the week following hope to be at home again.

Faithfully & Ever Yours,
Elihu Burritt

MS. LETTERS FROM ELIHU BURRITT
American Peace Society

New Britain, Sept. 23/73

[Rev J B Miles]

My Dear Friend

I am very anxious to hear from you and hope to do so in a few days. I feel deeply the very trying circumstances in which you go to Europe this time, owing to the Ghent scheme.[43] Really I think it was very dishonorable in him to attempt to head you off when you had prepared the way for a great meeting of jurists. I most earnestly hope he will not succeed in this attempt. I have written a very earnest letter to Mr Woolsey, urging him to put aside all matters that can possibly be postponed and represent America in the Congress at Brussels. He has written to Mr Field urging him to go to Ghent and try to prevent the meeting there from conflicting with yours. I hope this unforseen and mortifying move on the part of the Ghent man will be overcome. But I hope soon to know how the field lies.

I am a little anxious to know how Henry Richard will feel and act in regard to the Brussels meeting. He made a grand and powerful speech, with all Cobden's logic and a higher eloquence still. His triumph is a glory to him & his country. I hope he will not feel that he is transferring any of that glory to another in co-operating heartily with you.

I learn that a day or part of a day is to be given to Arbitration at the Evangelical Alliance. Rev Dr Boardman of Auburn, N. Y. is to read a paper, and probably Mr Woolsey will take part. I mean to go over and make a short speech if permitted. So I hope we shall have a popular Peace Congress in New York, if not at the Hague.

---

[43] M. Rolin Jacquemyns, editor-in-chief of *La Révue de droit international*, encouraged by Bluntschli and Francis Lieber, called a conference of experts on international law, which met at Ghent in 1873. The meeting resulted in the formation of the Institut de Droit International, the personnel and program of which was more restricted than that of the Association for the Reform and Codification of the Laws of Nations, which was formed in October, 1873, as a result of the campaign of Miles and Burritt.

I have finished my chapel and we have had services in it two Sundays. It seats about three hundred. Hope to have more leisure soon. I should like to spend a week in New York to interest the Alliance in the Peace Cause.

Yours Ever & Truly
Elihu Burritt

MS. LETTERS FROM ELIHU BURRITT
American Peace Society

New Britain, Ct. Nov. 28/73

My dear Friend Miles.

If I have not written you I have thought of you daily ever since you left, and no man in the world has rejoiced at your glorious success more sincerely than I. I thought it likely that you would return to the U. S. soon after the Brussels congress, and that a letter would miss you if I wrote after the meeting closed. Besides I have been doing Irishman's work nearly ten hours a day for several months on my chapel building. But I will waste no more time on explanation. Truly you have won a great triumph and a great crown of glory in your wonderful success, and I am almost glad I was not with you to share it with you; for you richly deserve it all, and I have had my share of what ever reputation attaches to a pioneer in former Congresses. Your work is the culmination of all the Am. Peace Society has tried to do for 30 years. I hope they will have grace and wisdom given them to recognise and appreciate this fact, though I feel some doubt of it. I wonder if you can realise all this success? You must think it a dream sometimes. How delighted I should have been to have made one of the company with you at Paris at the banquet after the Congress! I am especially delighted that Henry Richard finally came into the movement so heartily. I was sure he would do so though late. He must have aided you much, with his prestige and influence at Brussels. I have just read that Mancini has brought forward the same proposition in the Italian Parliament, and that both H. Richard and Mr Field were there to listen to his speech and witness his success. Were you not there too? I am glad you are to remain a while in Europe; that is the practical field for you—to work up the movement to its consummation. I am glad you have appointed another Congress of jurists—and provided for yearly meetings This is my old idea. I labored with Richard for nearly twenty years to have an annual Peace Congress somewhere, but could not move him.

I thank you for remembering me at Paris. It was deeply interesting to me to feel that my old friends Garnier and Passy were with you. I wish you would ask Passy if he ever received a letter from me enclosing a cheque for £2 and my photograph.—For myself I have not been idle. I have written to the N. Y. Tribune about the Brussels Congress, giving facts you sent me. I have also been writing with my utmost force to stem the war fever about this wretched Cuban affair. My letters to the N. Y. World & Conn. Courant have excited some thought in the public mind. Pres. Woolsey has done nobly, bringing out his views strongly against war with Cuba Sumner & Garrison have done the same, and Whittier too. So, I think the matter will be settled by arbitration or negotiation. But our military authorities have been for war, and the preparations will probably cost 30 millions extra.

I have received the Lond Peace Herald which gives a full and excellent summary of the Brussels congress. I hope our people will contribute something to the support of the cause. They have always been niggardly in regard to it. I have built myself poor, and have nothing to give just now. Money is terribly tight here. Our shoddy money has brought a general collapse in business, but hope we have touched bottom and will begin to rise again.

My Laymen's Union Chapel is a success; we have about 200 of all denominations present on Sunday 3 P. M service.

Now do please write me as often as you can, for no one in America delights more to hear of your progress.

Faithfully & Ever Yours,
Elihu Burritt

MS. LETTERS FROM ELIHU BURRITT
American Peace Society

St. John, N. B., Dec. 18, 1873

Dear Charles Sumner,

By all the noble and glorious sympathies and affinities that have identified your life with every good cause, I want to appeal to you to throw yourself "into the breach once more" & stem the flood of this new war spirit that is hurrying Congress into this senseless increase of the navy and other war-expenditures. You know well the history of war panics in England,[44]—how they have saddled on the necks of the people a constantly increasing burden for army & navy. Every flurry of the war-spirit, however brief, results in a new and permanent burden which the nation can never throw off. Thus in twenty years the expenditures have increased by *one third*. But that is nothing compared with the growth of our burdens from the same cause. Our expenditures for the army and navy since 1861 have *trebled* in this *last year of peace* before the Cuban question came up. And now when our country is taxed to the water's edge, this last blast of passion threatens to put a new burden upon us.

Why should the navy be increased? Of what earthly use has it been, aside from the Civil War, for 30 years? The only duty that gives it a *raison d'être*, it has neglected to perform, & that derelection of duty has brought about this imbroglio with Spain.[45] If our ship *Kansas* had brought the

[44] See Richard Cobden, "The Three Panics; an Historical Episode," in *The Political Writings of Richard Cobden* (London, 1868), Vol. II, pp. 209 ff.

[45] The *Virginius*, an American registered vessel carrying men and supplies to the Cuban insurgents, was captured by the Spanish war vessel *Tornado*.

Virginius back to the United States, to be tried in our courts, as the Spanish captain requested, that vessel would have been estopped in her filibustering career, and we should have been spared all this trouble and expense. If our Navy has any earthly use and duty it is to prevent the prostitution of our flag by pirates, slavers, or filibusterers.

But I need not appeal to any such considerations. You know all and feel all that can be urged against this insane endeavor to increase our peace armament, which cost three times today what it did in 1861.

I am spending a fortnight in these Provinces, but I could not resist the desire to write to you on this important subject.

Ever & Faithfully Yours,
Elihu Burritt

SUMNER MSS., *Letters Received, Foreign,* Vol. CL
Harvard College Library

New Britain, Feb. 18/74

[Rev. J. B. Miles]
My Dear Friend.

I see by the resolutions passed at the meeting of the Peace Society that they fully understand and appreciate your work abroad. Whatever they may be willing and able to do, I think you must form an International Code Council or Association, with its center & head in New York. This it seems to me, must be your first and immediate work. It must be a *national* work, with one or more influential men from each state. I am willing to do what I can to help you. I am pressed today, so can write no more now.

Yours faithfully & Ever
Elihu Burritt

MS. LETTERS FROM ELIHU BURRITT
American Peace Society

The execution of fifty-three of the passengers and crew was, under the circumstances, without excuse, and the incident threatened to end in a war between the United States and Spain.

New Britain, March 10/74

[Rev. J. B. Miles]
My Dear Friend.

I had closed my letter before yours came to hand. I do feel very anxious about your position, for I cannot bear the thought of your retiring to a pulpit and leaving the great work which you have carried forward within arms reach of a glorious consummation. Now it seems to me that your next move should be to form an International Code Association, by which you can enlist a new set of men altogether, who will appreciate the work and sustain it. Of course New York must be the headquarters of such an Association, and you must be the working & inspiring spirit of it. To form such an association will be easy for you after what you have done in Europe. Now suppose you go on to New York and set yourself to work in this mission? I think Robert Lindley Murray, Pres of the Nat. Friends Peace Society will help you, give you names to call upon etc. There is also Mr Willitts, whom you know, and Dr Crosby would be a strong man.

You would then have a new cause of appeal for funds based on a different standpoint. I hope you will go on with the full preparation and intention to make it the business of a full month if need be. You cannot think of doing it in a day or even a week or fortnight. If you could bring on your family to New London or to some quiet town on the Sound, where living, rent etc. are cheap, while you are operating in New York, you could feel easier in regard to expense. I hope your personal friends will help you just through this crisis, for times must change for the better soon.

For myself, I feel I am pretty much "played out." I have built myself out of funds, and I am quite ashore as to giving or spending anything for the cause just now. What I can do with my pen *here*, I will do gladly. My health is precarious and I do not like to go from home. When you go to New York, you must come this way, that we may make up a programme together

Yours Ever & Truly
Elihu Burritt

MS. LETTERS FROM ELIHU BURRITT
American Peace Society

New Britain, May 20/74.

[Rev. J. B. Miles]
My Dear Friend

I am very glad indeed, to hear of your success in New York & Washington. Really I congratulate you on the good fortune that attends your movements at home and abroad. I am sure nothing will tempt you to leave the important mission you have in hand.

You have inaugurated a great movement, which must result in a new departure and a new future for the nations. I wish I could help you. But I have had my turn and my day in the work. You must increase but I must decrease and subside into silence or inactivity.

I am especially glad you have raised so much money in New York. I felt confident that you would find the sinews of war there. I hope you will keep up the most intimate correspondence and intercourse with the leading men of that city —that you will go there as often as possible & write to them and keep them advised of all your movements & plans, and impress them with your confidence in their sympathy and support.

I will write to Schurz and hope he will take Sumner's place in the movement. He is just the man to do it—nearly the only man on the Repub. side in the Senate in whom I have full confidence.

I cannot be with you this time, at your Anniversary. I feel my speaking days are done. Besides, I feel rather poor in purse, having spent my money or resources too freely the past year. So that the expense of a trip to Boston or New

York would be a burden to me. I am also very busy with my philological work, hoping to finish it this month for the press. It is just possible I may go to England for 3 months this summer, but it is uncertain, depending upon health, etc.

Do keep me advised of your movements.

Yours Truly & Ever
Elihu Burritt

MS. LETTERS FROM ELIHU BURRITT
American Peace Society

New Britain. May 27/74

[Rev. J. B. Miles]
My Dear Friend

Don't give up the ship that you are bringing into a glorious haven. You know how I feel in regard to the Boston *regime*. It is a great drag upon you, and no help. You can make the International Code Committee a great power, and guide it, and it will yield you ample support. So I hope you may shift your position to New York as champion of that movement and let the Am. Peace Society take care of itself. But don't think of retiring to a pulpit, where you would be as it were lost to the world—or to the grandest enterprise of the age.

In Haste Yours

Elihu Burritt.

MS. LETTERS FROM ELIHU BURRITT
American Peace Society

New Britain, June 10/74

Rev J. B. Miles D. D.
Dear Friend

I have just finished my great philological work, embraced Grammars, Reading and Parsing Lessons and Vocabularies, in Sanskrit, Hindustani, Persian and Turkish and I hope now to breath a little more freely.

I have but just received the London Peace Herald for *May* containing my letter to Richard! As I have not said anything to the public on his motion, or on Charles Sumner, I should be glad if you would publish it in your next Advocate. If you do so, will you please correct a bad mistake and say "exciting *monument* of the strife" instead of *movement*. If you will do me another favor I shall be greatly obliged. Although I have written twice to Lee & Shepard, I cannot get a word from them about my book. In my last I asked if they could let me have a little money to go to England with early in July. But they do not send me a word. Now I wish you would call and ask as if accidentally or on your own part as a friend, how the book has sold, and if they have been satisfied with the sale. Please don't imply that you ask at my request. I should like to know if any considerable interest has been manifested in the book, and if it has gone to the general trade.

I have received a letter from *Worcester*, enquiring who are the publishers and where it may be had; also a letter from New York, asking the same question.

Do write me soon and tell me how it is with you.

Ever and Truly Yours
Elihu Burritt

MS. LETTERS FROM ELIHU BURRITT
American Peace Society

New Britain, June 27/74

Dear Mr Miles

I send a little tribute to the memory of dear Visschers, which I think our Committee would be willing to adopt.

I have thought much of that invidious Ghent movement that is cutting in ahead of us. This last step is worse than the first. They will go in first to Geneva and absorb all the interest, and take off all the cream. They will have Pres. Woolsey's papers written expressly for them. They will have all its capital of credit. We shall have it second hand —and sit down to the crumbs of the second table. I feel fairly indignant at their stolen march and stolen thunder. I really wish we could meet at *Berne* or *Turin*, to get rid of this "Old Man of the Mountain" that threatens to ride on our shoulders all over Europe. Don't you think you could manage to change the place of meeting from Geneva to Berne, or Turin?

Another thing: We did a great mistake in not inviting Henry Barnard [46] to go as a delegate. He made the first peace speech in Connecticut. His family are now in Geneva, and he will be there at the time of the meeting. I saw him yesterday morning, and think he felt the omission of his appointment So I hope you will add his name to the list of delegates without fail.

He suggested a matter of great importance to Pres. Woolsey—that as he had written a paper for Ghent on the Impracticability of the Three Rules, that he should write *another* paper for *us* at Geneva on Three Rules, embracing the same objects, which would be practicable and right to his own mind. Now this would be worth all the rest of the delegation to Geneva from America. As it is, we shall have nothing from him there except what comes through the crumbs that fall from the Ghent man's table. Now will you not second Mr Barnards proposition to him? Will you not write him, begging him to write such a paper for us?

I hope you will be able to get off as soon as possible. If you are not there it will all be a dead failure. I wish you could start by the middle of July. You will have to canvass among the publicists and button-hole them and almost lead them by the collar to Geneva or to the congress.

For my part, everything is uncertain. If my health holds up to the work I intend to go, but cannot be with you in preliminary work, but should hope to be with you a week before the meeting.

Write me soon and tell me how it is with you; If funds

---

[46] Henry Barnard (1811-1900), distinguished educator. For his views on peace see M. E. Curti, *Social Ideas of American Educators* (N. Y., 1935), pp. 139-140.

cannot be raised by contribution we must get some friend to lend you $1200 or $1500.

Ever Yours
Elihu Burritt

MS. LETTERS FROM ELIHU BURRITT
American Peace Society

New Britain, Ct. July 22/74

My Dear Friend

I am an unfortunate man. I had packed up things to leave for England, when my old ailment came on me so severely that I had to telegraph to Montreal to say that I could not go on Saturday's steamer. The doctor thinks I shall rally from it, and I feel better today, and still hope I may get off by Aug. 1. I want to go exceedingly, but when my poor turns come on, I shrink from being away from home, on the sea or in a foreign land. How happy & grateful you should be that you are in the vigor of health and middle manhood for this great work! I hope you will be strong and of good courage for the campaign. Let me again suggest that you make Henry Barnard helpful to you in preparing for the Congress. I suppose he will be in Geneva by the time you are. Also Mr Hubbard will help you about writing copying and outside work.

How is [it] about the Advocate? I have not yet received the July No, nor of the Angel. Do drop me a line before you leave, and give me your European address. I have now written three letters since I received your last. Wishing you every blessing, I am

Ever Yours Truly
Elihu Burritt

P. S. I have just received your letter and am glad you have overcome money difficulty about going. Do get off as soon as possible. If I continue to improve I hope to sail Aug. 1.

MS. LETTERS FROM ELIHU BURRITT
American Peace Society

New Britain, Ct. Oct. 3/74.

[Rev. J. B. Miles]

My Dear Friend

No, I can hardly realise that you are "home again from a foreign shore"—that all this great work has been done in two months, counting in the two voyages across the Atlantic. It seems impossible. Well I congratulate you most heartily. Did we think on that stormy Sabbath at New Bedford, that our programme thus sketched would result in such an issue? All your life put together has not made such a mark on the world, as your last two years in this great cause.

Well now we must impress upon the American mind a sense of the vast importance of the victory already won, and of the victories still & soon accessible. It strikes me a series of public meetings to ratify and commemorate the Geneva Conference should be held, beginning with one in New York with Mr Field chairman, to be followed by other meetings in the chief cities. If life and strength suffice I will go with you, or attend a meeting in New York. You should take time to get up these meetings,—say on the first of November to begin with.

Now don't press yourself for time, but take enough of it to prepare well and give others a chance to prepare. I think the next evening after a conference of the Code Committee would be a good time for a public meeting in Cooper Institute or elsewhere. Suppose you write to Mr Field on the subject. I think he would approve of it, and be glad to preside at such a meeting, which is his place.

I want to see you and have plenty of time to talk over the whole matter with you. Can you not stop over a day here on your way to New York? I am much better than I was when I started for Europe the 25th of July—am very busy with mission work by night and philology by day. I am short and crowded for means just now and cannot make long or expensive journies, but hope to be easier in November. Lee & Shepard have not deigned to notice my letters, and hardly expect to get anything from them. I intend to write to some of the authors whose works they publish, to ask if they are treated so, or whether an exception is made to my disfavor. Do Write Soon.

Ever Truly Yours
Elihu Burritt

MS. LETTERS FROM ELIHU BURRITT
American Peace Society

New Britain, Ct. Nov. 9/74

Rev. J. B. Miles D. D.
My Dear Friend

I am glad and grateful that I may write with my own hand my thanks to you for your very good and kind words of sympathy received on a bed of prostration. I am very thankful that I have rallied to reading and writing strength, which is all I can expect to recover for a long time to come. I hope I may yet with great care, be able to do a little more for our great cause with pen if not with voice.

Do write me often and tell me your plans and progress. Are you going to have any ratification meetings to commemorate your success at Geneva? I hope you will be in free and frequent communication with the friends & coworkers in Europe, to keep them up to the work.

I have never heard a word from Lee and Shepard in regard to my book. They do not deign to notice my two last letters. If you can do it easily and naturely, I wish you would drop in upon them casually and inquire as my friend, if my book continues to sell at a satisfactory rate. It has been noticed very favorably abroad. I do feel that they must have made a very special exception to my disfavor— that they cannot have treated other author's so, whose works they have published.

Will you not be coming this way soon? I long to see you and am now able to see friends when they call.

Ever & Faithfully Yours
Elihu Burritt

MS. LETTERS FROM ELIHU BURRITT
American Peace Society

New Britain, Ct., Dec. 1. 74.

Rev. J. B. Miles D. D.

Dear Friend

I cannot of course attend your meeting in New York on Thursday next, which I much regret, for few meetings can be held in this country of greater importance. You and I think alike on the subject and I wish you to act and speak for me in the Council. From my long experience with French, Germans and other continental men I have long ago learned what you have learned more recently, that their enthusiasm needs to be mixed with the solid *staying* power of the Anglo-Saxon faith, courage and tenacity.—They must be held up to an even work by this union with English and American pluck and backbone. It will not be safe to leave them long without the steady backing of these elements of moral power. Therefore, I hope the International Code Committee will inaugurate measures that shall not only impress the public mind in this country with a sense of what the movement has realised already and what it is yet to attain, but which shall keep up a working interest in the Continental allies and associations, and tend to hold them to the work. It seems to me that a series of public meetings beginning at New York, to ratify the proceeding at Geneva would not only raise up new friends of the cause in America but also strengthen the friends in Continental Europe. I am sure that something will result from your deliberations which will give the movement a new impulse.

Yours Very Truly,
Elihu Burritt

P. S.   David A. Wells, of Norwich, Ct. the Richard Cobden of America, has written me for a copy of Charles Sumner's *"True Grandeur of Nations."* Will you kindly see that a copy is sent him by post forthwith?

E. B.

MS. LETTERS FROM ELIHU BURRITT
American Peace Society

New Britain, Conn. Jan 4/75

Dear Mr Miles

I write a few lines by return of post, to say that I hope you will keep up heart and hope under this pressure of untoward circumstances. The times must change ere long, as all good causes are water logged just now. I do sympathise with you most sincerely in your trials with stupidity and pigheaded prejudice. You must feel yourself *alone*, with no one in your Committee you can lean upon. I still wish you could either settle down in New York or be there full half of your time. You would find a different set of men there to sympathise and cooperate with you—men of means, of mind, heart & soul, who could understand your work and say *we* [are] with you in it. It is to my mind quite certain, that you will have to give yourself more and more completely to the *International* Code movement. That is the great and almost only practical work connected with the peace cause now and hereafter. The writing and distribution of tracts on the abstract principle, which hardly a member of your Committee holds, does but little good. Now New York is the centre and capital and source of the International Code movement. The President is there and the Secretary should be there. I am confident if you were there you would enlist a great number of influential and wealthy men; that you would find means to support you and the work. Then why not go there and try it for a month at least? You can do this without dissolving your connection with the Am Peace Society at once. But I forsee that you will have to cut loose from them. They are a dead weight upon you; if they were in sympathy with you and your work but could not otherwise help you, there might be some reason for standing by them. But they give you neither sympathy nor salary. Why then do you feel bound to Boston? Suppose you go on to New York and canvas for a week at least? Form a State Peace Society as a feeder and auxiliary to the International Code Association? But without such a society, the Code Assoc. is large enough to employ and support you without outside help. I suppose you will not publish my article for many weeks if at all, so I wish you would send it back to me by post.

Yours Faithfully,
Elihu Burritt

MS. LETTERS FROM ELIHU BURRITT
American Peace Society

New Britain, Jan 25. 1875

[Miss Hattie Butler, New Britain]
Dear Miss Butler,

I met your sister the other day, when it occurred to me for the first time that I had not invited you to join the class of young ladies who come here every Saturday evening to study *Sanskrit*. I am sorry that I forgot you when I proposed the study to them, for it would have given me especial pleasure to have had the grand-daughter of one of my old neighbors in the class. They are making very good progress, and constitute probably the only class of ladies in America or Europe taking lessons in the language, which is the mother of our own and perhaps elder sister of Greek & Latin. The knowledge of it is necessary to a thorough acquaintance with our own language, or any other in Europe. Now I write to say, that I should be very much pleased if you would join the class, and I would give you two or three private lessons to bring you up even with the rest. You need no books, and would be at no other expense than an hour's time one evening a week. The ladies of the class are Miss Mary Stanley, Miss Julia Francis, Marion Ellis, Miss Comstock, Miss Gibbs, Miss Mary Brown, and I think you will like them as they will you.

Should you accept this invitation I should be happy to give you a few separate or private lessons on any evenings or days convenient to you.

Yours Sincerely,
Elihu Burritt

BURRITT MSS.
Library of the Institute of New Britain

New Britain, Conn. May 27/75

Rev J. B. Miles D. D.
My dear Friend

I thank you for your kind letter, and for the invitation to attend the Congress at The Hague. My spirit is willing enough to go, but my flesh is too weak for such a voyage and enterprise. You know the nature and severity of my attack last Fall, and that it would not be safe for me to make such a journey when liable to a return of the same most serious ailment. But I have thought I might prepare a short paper which might be read at the meeting, or published in connection with its proceedings. I should be very glad to prepare such a paper, if you think it would do any good. I would not make it more than 15 minutes long.

I hope you will get off as early as you can, for you are and must be the inspiring spirit of the whole. You ought to be in Europe half the time, until a great result is reached.

I should like to know if the Ghent man appointed his meeting at the Hague *before* you or *after* you. Cannot you manage next time to cut loose from him? He swallowed you up by cutting in before you, and the world will never be able to recognise yours as an independent organisation until you meet at a different place and time. Do try to cut loose from him this time or at the next meeting after the Hague.

If you should meet in London, perhaps you can there establish your independence. I think it would [be] best for you, not to appoint the time and place of the next meeting, when you close at the Hague, but leave the selection to a committee representing the International Law Association, who will decide, say within 3 months after the Hague meeting.

Let the Ghent man fix upon the time and place for his meeting, *first*, then you will have a wide field before you to steer clear of him.

I hope you will call here before you go.

Ever Yours Sincerely
Elihu Burritt

MS. LETTERS FROM ELIHU BURRITT
American Peace Society

New Britain Conn.
May 10, 1877

[To Joseph Cooper [47]]

My Dear Friend,

Although I was so glad to hear from you, I was sorry, indeed, to learn that you were so unwell as to be unable to write yourself without fatigue. I sincerely hope that it is only a temporary ailment.

I do not wonder that you and all the friends of Peace in England are distressed at this new thunderburst of war on the old Eastern Question. Indeed the conflict between the Turkish race and civilization seems irrepressible. Since You wrote, it has entered upon a new phase, and even is already at its terrible work of blood and iron. It is too late for mediation or arbitration. Yesterday we had the telegraphic news that the Sultan has donned the authority of Mahomet and sounded the tocsin of a holy war; that both in Europe and Asia the Russian and Turkish armies engaged in daily bat-

---

[47] Joseph Cooper (1800-1881), a Quaker philanthropist and honorable secretary of the Bristol and Foreign Antislavery Society.

tles. So nothing seems left but to await the verdict of the sword. It would be utterly in vain for the United States to offer its mediation at this crisis, for if Turkey would not listen to the united voice of the great European Powers, but rejected it with almost contempt, she would not regard any overture from the American Republic now in the frenzy of her fanaticism.

If our Government or people could do anything towards holding back England from again fighting to uphold "the integrity and independence of the Ottoman Empire," I earnestly wish it could be done. Now I believe it is an empire that has had its probation—that it has been proved and found wanting of every element of moral or political vitality—that like other nations that have died of heart disease, the Turkish dominion must disappear, though the Turkish people continue to live under a new regime.

You know my thoughts on this subject, which are the same now as twenty years ago. I do most earnestly hope that the Turkish party in England will not be able to drag the country into another war for the perpetuation of the Ottoman rule. Neither England nor any outside Powers can prevent it. Indeed, they must believe that this end will come sometime; that Constantinople, after five hundred years' subjection to Mohammedan dominion, must revert to the occupation of a Christian Power. Some Christian Power must possess it that is able to recover the countries or regions around it from the deadly abuse of Turkish rule. To my mind Russia is the only Power situated and able to perform this mission. I wish that England could acquiesce with this condition—that she would take Egypt and let Russia have Turkey. She cannot always be fighting or watching Russia with a hostile eye. The end must come—she knows it. Why not let it come now, and accept the situation, and have done forever with this everlasting Eastern Question?

My health is very feeble, but I never was busier with my pen. I have written many articles on this Eastern Question, and sent one yesterday to a New York paper on the subject. I feel almost left alone, now that Amasa Walker and J. B. Miles and nearly all the old workers are gone. But I intend to work for the cause to the last.

Ever and truly yours,

Elihu Burritt

Herald of Peace, new series, No. 326 (June 1, 1877), p. 251

[New Britain, Conn. no date]

[To Henry Richard,
    Secretary of the English Peace Society]

God grant that you may be able to stand at this day of crucial trial. Gladstone is a tower of strength, and Bright and other men of power will stand by you, and with them a host of men of heroic courage athwart the course of a warlike Government. How anxiously I shall wait for the issue of this struggle between the two great forces of English sentiment, which will now be so sharply defined and arrayed against each other in the severest antagonism! If the friends of Peace can win a victory now over such a war-power, it will be a lasting and glorious triumph. If England can be held back this time, it will be a new point of hopeful departure for mankind.

I feel an interest in this Eastern Question aside from that of Peace and War. I feel affected by anything that touches the honour of England, or the place she should hold in the estimation of the civilised world. With this reverence for her history and character, I read with pain the frank and repeated declaration that she recognises only "British interests" in her position on this Eastern Question; that the rights and condition of the oppressed Christian populations under Turkish rule do not affect her, nor move her to pity or sympathy; that she will not allow any nation to rescue them from that yoke, if the independence of the Ottoman empire is endangered by such interference. It seems like having vested interests in a nightmare, or a drought, or a pestilence, to have any interests worth fighting for in such an abomination of desolation. It was the bitterest experience of the Free States in the time of American Slavery that it was put in the bond of the Fugitive Slave Bill that we should deliver up the slave to the slave-hunter who pursued him to our highest places of freedom. It was in the bond, and it was an iron that entered red hot into the souls of freemen. How sad, how incongruous with the antecedents of England, that she should willingly enter into a Fugitive-Nation Bond, binding herself to send back to Turkish slavery the oppressed nationalities fleeing to a sympathising neighbour for refuge,—that she should even do blood-hound service for the unspeakable Turk to this end!

I shall watch every phase of the movement of the English mind at this stage of the struggle with the deepest interest. I know that all man dare do, you will do, to stem the warward current. Be strong and of good courage.

Ever yours faithfully,
Elihu Burritt

Herald of Peace, Vol. XVI (Apr. 1, 1878), no. cccxxxiv.

New Britain, Conn. Nov. 30/77.

Rev. C. H. Malcolm, D. D.[48]
My Dear Sir:

I am very glad to hear from you, and to know that you were again in the country after your visit to Europe. I read with great interest your leader in the Advocate on the Antwerp Congress, and I am sure that you will look back to that assembly as to one of the most memorable of your life. I was certain that you would bring back a deeper impression of the great movement which Dr Miles set on foot by this indefatigable zeal, activity and enthusiasm. And he

---

[48] The Rev. Charles Malcolm, D. D., was corresponding secretary of the American Peace Society from 1876-1880, having succeeded Mr. Miles on his death in 1876.

did all this as representative of the American Peace Society, and against their wish and will and in face of their opposition. He connected the Society with the most powerful and important international organisation ever formed for the well being of mankind. You must have felt this at Antwerp, and what it was and is to succeed him in the great position he left you to fill. And I earnestly hope you will make it the mission of your future life to fill it "without variableness or shadow of turning," or flagging of faith or weariness in effort. You see what manner of men you are associated with in this great movement; what grand objects it embraces and the moral and intellectual forces it has enlisted for the realisation of these ends. You saw how the steam-ship companies appreciated and honored your position and mission. I earnestly hope that you will take up the work of Dr Miles just where he left it and do all he would have done for the cause if he had lived. It seems to me that you must feel that this position is one of greater importance, dignity and power than the pastorship over a single church or congregation. There are a thousand ministers well fitted to fill successfully the pulpit, where there is one to fill with the right heart, and faith and hope the position you have assumed.

I sympathise with you as deeply as I did with Dr Miles in regard to the lack of support you receive from the American Peace Society. I still see no reasonable hope of a change for the better except from a change in the *locale* of the Society. I believe it can never be regarded as national and receive national support while its head-center is in Boston. I wish you could see it in this light, and be encouraged to prepare the way for this change, and hope that you will begin forthwith the preliminary steps towards this end. I think you can do this without creating any unpleasant sensibility in the Boston circle. Nothing can be more legitimate, proper and necessary in the scope of your duties and labors as Secretary than to form auxiliary societies as branches of the mother society. Now then I would suggest that you should reorganise the New York Peace Society which existed in Father Ladd's day; that you go to New York City for this purpose, and work up such a Society, enlisting one by one as a committee large-hearted and generous men who will contribute liberally when they see a practical end in view. I would proceed with great care and caution, and not depend upon influential names. My programme would be this— That you should get from Philadelphia *Friends* the Addresses of Friends in New York most likely to sympathise and cooperate; that you should then go to New York allowing you plenty of time to operate there; that you should call upon these Friends one by one and explain fully the great work you have in hand, dwelling upon the International Code Association as only one of the Agencies the Peace Society has originated for abolishing war. You can truthfully say and urge this for it was the work of Dr Miles who represented the Peace Society and was its only working power, though it is not entitled to the honor he won for it. When you have enlisted the steady, unswerving Quaker element for half of the committee, I would carefully canvas for liberal and influential laymen of other denominations for the other half—such men as Wm E. Dodge & the like. When you have got a dozen to act as a committee you can easily effect an organisation at a public meeting however small. Then it would be natural and necessary that you should remain to guide the new Society, to act as its honorary Secretary. It would need a local institution as well as name—an office which you would naturally occupy. From this point you could bring a new and vast field into the movement. Soon through your zeal and activity the new Society would draw in more contributions than the Boston Society and would become the most important of the two, and would most deserve and require your leadership. The publication of the Peace Herald would naturally be transferred to New York, where it was first issued, and that would be as it ought to be the centre of a National Society. You could there keep up your connection with the International Code more fully. Indeed you ought to be Secretary of the American Branch of the Code Association as well as of the American Peace Society, and be to it all that Dr Miles was. I fear A. P. Sprague [49] has not heart, faith hope and enthusiasm enough for the position. I fear he is doing nothing to make an interest for the movement. I wish you could see him when in New York and find out what manner of man he is, whether he is doing anything or proposing to do anything for the cause. I wish you could get from him my paper, which was read at Philadelphia and which I prepared chiefly to show that the International Code Movement originated entirely with the Peace Society. I hope you will never let the public forget this connection.

I have written you a long letter, but only a tithe of what I should like to say to you face to face. My health is very feeble, and I am confined to my house, but hope you may be able to call on me when returning to Boston.

Ever yours sincerely,
Elihu Burritt

MS. LETTERS FROM ELIHU BURRITT
American Peace Society

New Britain, Conn., March 17th, 1876

[To George Drury [50]]

Dear Sir:—

My health has been declining for some time, so that I cannot expect to get away from home again. With regard to the proposition of the workingmen [to forge weapons of war into useful implements of peace during the Centennial Ex-

---

[49] A. P. Sprague, of Troy, New York, had recently won a prize offered in a competition for the best essay on an international code.

[50] George Drury was a member of the Workingman's Association of Philadelphia.

position, as propaganda for the cause] I fear it might *burlesque* the Peace cause if carried out. For there were never so many furnaces, forges and arsenals at work, turning out the latest improvements in the machinery of war, as at the present moment, and no mind and hand more busy and ingenious in the invention and manufacture of such weapons than the American. Against a few old bayonets turned to peaceful implements at Philadelphia, you will see the machinery of war having a central show in the great Exhibition. If the friends of Peace can do anything to prevent or lessen this show of reaping-machines of war, they would effect more for the cause than beating a few obsolete weapons into plowshares or pruninghooks. I read that it is proposed to bring up the old Macedonian frigate, captured in the last war, as an interesting relic, especially to our British guests. I fully expect that a hundred other mementoes of our wars with England and at home will be paraded at the Centennial to show the nice perception of "the eternal fitness of things," which even the leaders of the great Anniversary entertained.

I do most earnestly hope that the grand occasion may really advance the cause of Peace and universal brotherhood, and I regret that I cannot expect to witness it with my own eyes. I feel that my work is done, but am glad that as old workers drop out of the ranks, new laborers take THEIR places with the vigor of hope and faith.

With best regards to yourself and all your fellow-workers,

I am faithfully yours

Elihu Burritt

The Voice of Peace, Vol. III (May 1876), pp. 28-29

❧

IN less than three years the learned blacksmith was dead. His work was only partly finished. But he died firm in the faith that others would fight on as he had fought to make the human spirit more free, and its earthly home a less unjust and a more kindly place. He realized, too, that his spiritual heirs would see new evils, and fight them as resolutely as he had fought those which his eyes and heart had discovered. And he would have said to them, as he said to his co-worker, Henry Richard, "Be strong and of good courage."